D0966432

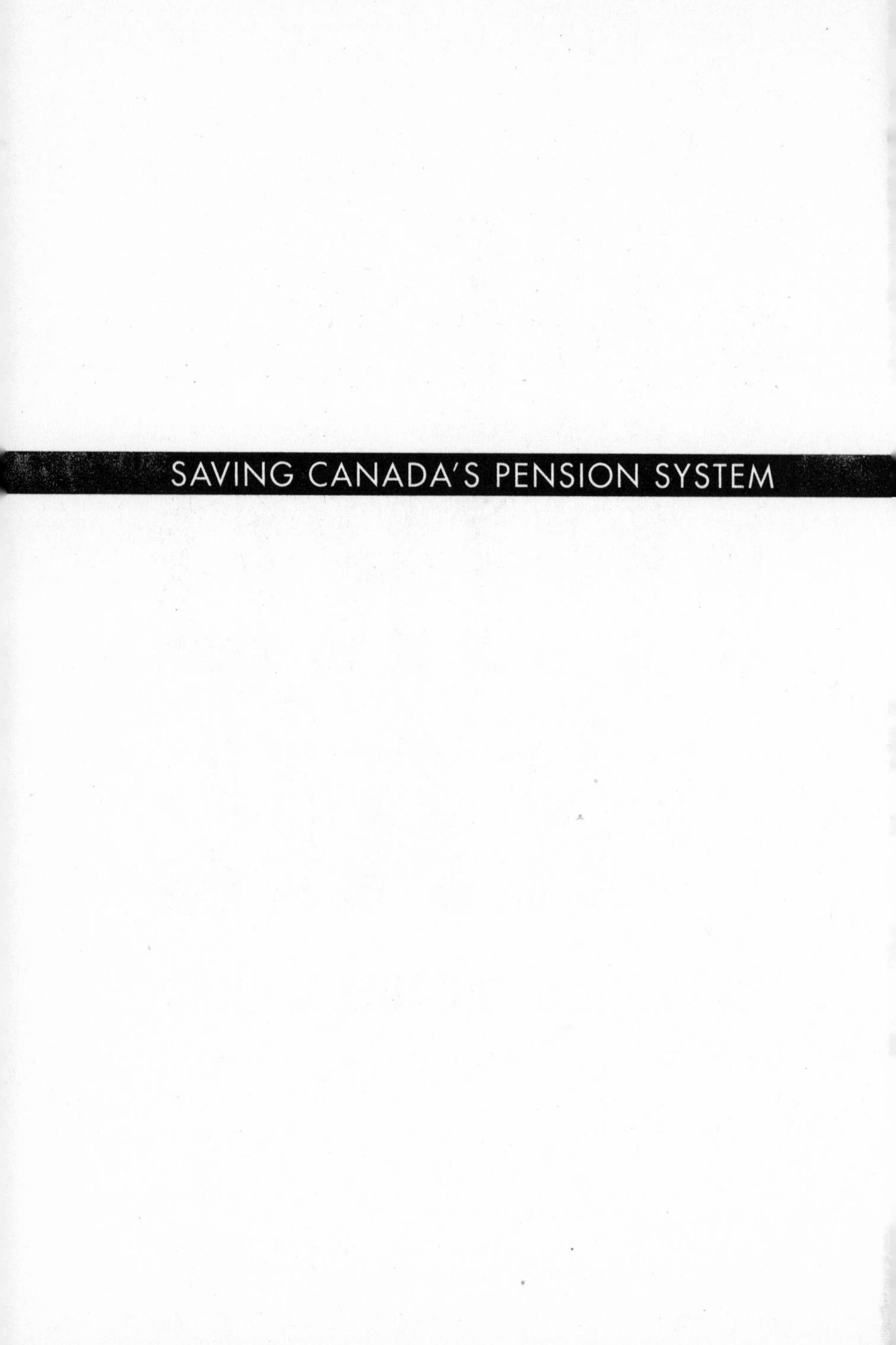

SAVING CANADA'S PENSION SYSTEM

THE THIRD RAIL

JIM LEECH & JACQUIE McNISH

Signal is an imprint of McClelland & Stewart, a division of Random House of Canada Limited, a Penguin Random House Company

The views and opinions expressed in this book are the personal views and opinions of the authors and do not necessarily reflect those of OTPP.

Library and Archives Canada Cataloguing in Publication data available upon request.

ISBN: 978-0-7710-4663-6

Printed and bound in the United States of America

McClelland & Stewart,
a division of Random House of Canada Limited,
a Penguin Random House Company
One Toronto Street
Suite 300
Toronto, Ontario
M5C 2V6

1 2 3 4 5 17 16 15 14 13

We dedicate this book to
our children and their children,
who deserve a better pension future

Jennifer Cumming, Joanna Thiessen, and Andrew Leech;
Cedar, Sydney, Travis, Aurora Joy, and Sky
—*Jim Leech*

Harry and Lewis Cole
—*Jacquie McNish*

CONTENTS

PROLOGUE

When everything is going right, it takes ten minutes for John Ferguson to drive south from his office in the suburb of Millidgeville to Saint John, New Brunswick. But everything was far from right on the afternoon of April 11, 2005. About twenty minutes after he had left work, ten spent worrying, Ferguson finally arrived at his destination near the Saint John harbour: the fifteen-floor cement bunker that houses City Hall. A broad-shouldered, muscular man of forty-one with close-cropped, mica-flecked hair, Ferguson clenched the steering wheel and stared at the cement wall housing his city government. "I can't do this," he said out loud, then threw his Pontiac Vibe in reverse and squealed off.

John Ferguson was afraid.

He hadn't felt this way since he was eleven, when, upon returning to live in Saint John after years away, the new kid in class found himself bullied. The first recess he was pushed to the ground, the next day it was a punch to the head. The hazing continued until his father noticed the cuts and instructed his son to fight back or stock up on bandages. "It was the start of four to five years of being in arguments," Ferguson remembers. So many that his high school principal gave him the nickname "Mr. Scrapper."

Ferguson comes from a long line of scrappers. His father is one of seventeen brothers and sisters from Tracadie, an Acadian town that never recovered from the collapse of timber. Hardship was a way of life. One great-grandfather was sliced in half by a mill saw. Fergusons made ends meet by erecting telephone poles, trapping, cutting hair, and selling dry goods. John Ferguson's grandfather ran a barbershop and a fleet of garbage trucks. "In our family it was felt you had to stand up and face things," Ferguson says.

As a teenager, Ferguson made his mark as a nimble, combative athlete, excelling in high school hockey and football. But it's one thing to battle middle linebackers and schoolyard bullies, quite another to fight the power-brokers of City Hall, and in the spring of 2005 John Ferguson found himself in the crosshairs of a brutal challenge to his professional career. Saint John wanted to silence him, and Ferguson knew enough about local politics to understand that the city's political establishment might cut a man in half faster than any New Brunswick sawmill.

How did a civic-minded jock end up facing public execution? Ferguson asks himself the same question. After graduating from high school, the ex-athlete landed a job as a recreation supervisor for a Saint John community centre. In 1996, the province hired him as a consultant to help other communities with local programs. In his spare time he played hockey, ran a weekend movie theatre, managed bike rodeos, and lobbied the city to invest in recreation. Such public-mindedness won him friends, and in 2004 he ran for city council to have more say in community programs.

Recreation projects weren't on tap when Ferguson sat down for his first council meeting in June 2004. One pressing bit of business for Mayor Ivan Court and the city's new council was approving trustees to the pension plan board, a $260 million fund that looked after the retirement accounts of 1,500 city workers and retirees. Reappointing the plan's experienced trustees, a senior city official warned, was vital because the fund had a multimillion-dollar deficit. Ferguson voted in favour of the proposed trustees – a mix of senior city staff, councillors, and local professionals – and shrugged off the deficit news. After all, he was a sports and rec guy.

Three months later, city councillors learned that the pension deficit was $44 million. Even to a layman like Ferguson, the number was stunning. Saint John was on the hook to replenish a pension deficit that amounted to nearly half the city's annual revenues. More remarkable was the council's reaction. "There was very little conversation," he says.

Ferguson began asking questions. What caused the deficit? How would the city replenish the shortfall? The more questions Ferguson asked, the more unpopular he became. Mayor Court brushed off his concerns. City managers told him he was overreacting. When Ferguson tabled a motion at a closed council meeting to appoint a committee to review the looming crisis, it was voted down. Later when council agreed to let him join a working group to study solutions, his proposal to issue a bond to pay for the deficit went nowhere.

Finally, in March 2005, Ferguson decided to sound the alarm. The trigger was a report in Saint John's daily newspaper, the *Telegraph-Journal*. According to a March 2 story, the city was six months late filing a devastating actuarial report outlining the pension deficit. Saint John was in a "legally precarious position" because an unusually high number of employees with questionable long-term disabilities had been allowed to take early retirement and collect full pensions. This, Ferguson figured, was the problem the city wanted to sweep under the rug.

As he drove around Saint John that April afternoon in 2005, worried for both his career and hometown,

Ferguson was apprehensive. He had planned to raise a stink about pensions that night at council. He had already quietly consulted with city officials, media, and union officials. A few days earlier, however, contacts warned against taking his fears public. It would cause a panic, make things worse.

After twenty minutes of fretful driving, Ferguson settled down. He'd chased away bullies before. Mr. Scrapper could do it again. "Come on, John," he said to himself, "you can do this." Pulling his Pontiac into a U-turn, Ferguson headed back to the city.

An hour later, he sat with fellow councillors at a horseshoe table on the first floor of City Hall. Shortly after the public session began he leaned into the microphone and started speaking from point-form notes. The notes were soon forgotten, however, and his voice grew louder, more emphatic. Saint John was facing a "severe" pension problem, he warned. There was lots of blame to go around, he said, jabbing his finger into the air. The plan was poorly managed, and some supervising trustees were conflicted because they were city employees who benefited from the plan. Worse still, he added, the pension board had been lax about allowing employees to use long-term disability claims to retire early with full benefits.

Ferguson spoke his piece in unvarnished New Brunswick English: "There is some serious shit coming down the sauna tube and some individuals in this room are at the wrong end of the sauna tube," he exclaimed. "I am told too, by senior legal counsel, there is standing evidence of gross negligence."

Shocked councillors chastised Ferguson for his harsh words. But no one challenged the details of his complaints at the meeting. Ferguson would keep the heat on for another twenty months. Strident and often uncertain about the intricacies of pension law and accounting rules, he railed against the pension plan trustees at council meetings and penned a column in a local newspaper, comparing Saint John pension woes to those of San Diego, a California city so hobbled by pension deficits that it was cutting school, library, and welfare programs.

Faced with a growing political furor, city officials and pension board directors huddled with lawyers. Paying off a multimillion-dollar pension deficit presented a city struggling with a shrinking population and high unemployment with hard choices: raise taxes, cut services, borrow money, or lower pension benefits. Elected officials in Saint John were staring at a political powder keg with a lit fuse. Alas, they aren't alone. Inadequate or unsustainable pensions represent a dire financial challenge that politicians secretly refer to as the third rail. Like the third high-voltage beam that powers subways, pension controversies are presumed to bring imminent destruction to any politician fool enough to touch them. Telling retirees, workers, and taxpayers that they must save more or trim benefits to save pension plans is a stand that requires enormous courage. Delay and denial is all too often the preferred political response to looming pension meltdowns.

Saint John waited until January 12, 2007, nearly two years after Ferguson's explosive outburst, before responding. When Ferguson left his Millidgeville office at the end of the day, a stranger approached him in the parking lot. Upon confirming Ferguson's name, the stranger handed him a thick envelope and retreated to his car. Ferguson returned to his office after he saw that the envelope contained a lengthy legal notice. He sat at his desk and read it with disbelief. The board of the city's pension fund, which included fellow councillors and city officials, was suing him for "a systemic and sustained course of action to maliciously and recklessly defame the Pension Board." Saint John was denying Ferguson's accusations.

The city wasn't going near the third rail. The Scrapper was now in for the fight of his life.

CHAPTER 1

CANADA'S PENSION PROMISE

Worn Out

Canada is a pension pioneer. Loyalist soldiers who fled to the Maritimes after the American Revolution received one of North America's first pensions in the early 1800s. Ottawa introduced pensions for civil servants in 1870, four decades ahead of a similar plan in the United States. The Grand Trunk Railway founded North America's first industrial pension plan for workers in 1874. And our banks began introducing employee pensions in the 1880s, several years ahead of their U.S. counterparts.

Early pensions bore little resemblance to modern-day benefits. In the nineteenth century, pensions were charity for the destitute. Benefits were threadbare and the qualifying process humiliating. New Brunswick passed an 1839 pension act for the relief of "old soldiers" of the Revolutionary War. Loyalist soldiers were surprisingly hardy, many living well into their eighties and a few beyond one hundred. Following Britain's longstanding tradition of rewarding its military with pensions, the colony belatedly agreed to come to the aid of former redcoats in their final years. In exchange for a petition that confirmed their loyal service to the King and "indigent circumstances," soldiers or their widows would receive £10 a year. These applications, now housed in the province's archives, are a litany of geriatric woe. "He is so decrepit and infirm as to be utterly unable to work," a friend of former soldier Barnet Manser, ninety-one, wrote in his 1838 petition to the Lieutenant-Governor. In another, Richard Jourdin's friend wrote: "He is now enfeebled by the iniquities of age and reduced to poverty and want."

Charity was Egerton Ryerson's motivation in 1853 when he convinced the government of Upper Canada to assist aging elementary schoolteachers.

Ryerson, chief superintendent of schools, secured an annual £500 grant for aging teachers who were "worn out in the service of their country." As Nelson Joannette documents in his doctoral thesis on early Canadian pensions, Ryerson's initial plan was to dole out small annual pensions equal to £6 for each year of service to elderly teachers. To qualify, teachers had to demonstrate they were "indigent," and "of good moral standing."[1] Ryerson's modest pension ambitions, however, were thwarted by a shortsightedness that would afflict future pension fund managers: he underestimated how much it would cost to fulfill his promise. He anticipated a few dozen teachers would be eligible for the pensions, but by 1858 more than 150 teachers had been approved. He was forced to award teachers only £2 for each year served – perhaps the first pension to adjust benefits because of funding challenges.

By the end of the century, pensions were gaining traction as a desirable employee perk. British employers began offering workplace pensions in the mid-1800s to tighten their hold on skilled factory hands during the Industrial Revolution. The plans were also an inducement for older, less efficient employees to move out to pasture. It was a British-owned company that introduced North America's first industrial pension plan. In 1874, U.K.–based owners of the Grand Trunk Railway, which ran through eastern Canada, began offering pensions to "inside" workers – clerks, telegraph operators, and passenger agents – to attract and motivate scarce skilled workers. By the early 1900s, Canada's major railways were offering pensions to most of their employees. Canada's banks, whose far-flung branches needed educated staff, were the next to introduce pensions. The Bank of Montreal led the way in 1885, and by the early 1900s employees at most Canadian banks could dream of earning an annual pension of more than $1,000, when they turned sixty-five.

Many early pension dreams were illusory. Workers usually had to work at a company for ten years before they were eligible to join pension programs. Employers had enormous discretion to yank the perks because they typically were the plans' sole contributors. If workers were disloyal, committed a felony, or declared bankruptcy, their pensions were usually suspended. Both the Grand Trunk Railway and Canadian Pacific Railway pulled pensions when workers joined legal strikes in the early 1900s.

The great irony about these conditional pensions is that during the first half-century of pensions most employees did not live long enough to collect their retirement bounty. When Grand Trunk introduced its first pension in 1874, average life expectancy was about fifty-five. The average worker had likely been dead for fifteen years before they were eligible to pocket pensions at the then retirement age of seventy. The perk cost so little that companies paid retirement cheques, like wages, out of operating expenses. These pay-as-you-go plans thrived until the Depression, when the harsh economic climate, coupled with declining death rates, prompted companies to rewrite their pension terms. By the 1930s, average life expectancies were catching up with retirement age: workers were actually living long enough to collect their pensions for at least a few years. Pensions were no longer a gift; they were a popular incentive that was starting to cost serious money.

Pensions were tightly controlled by employers in their first century. Governments and businesses decided who was worthy, what was paid, and who could be expelled from pension plans. In their second century, the pendulum swung the other way as pensions were seized upon by unions as a vital benefit that could be negotiated in contract talks. Pensions entered the hurly-burly of collective bargaining in the booming postwar era when the United Automobile Workers (UAW) won a lengthy quest to include pension payments in employment contracts with Detroit automakers. The first pension plan was included in contract talks with General Motors (GM) in 1950. Against a backdrop of frequent industry strikes, GM believed it had secured five years of labour peace when it agreed to add a fixed pension of $125 a month to workers' compensation packages.

In what became known as "The Treaty of Detroit," GM executives congratulated themselves for restoring predictability to the booming industry.[2] But as Peter Drucker warned in his prescient 1976 classic, *The Unseen Revolution*, what GM had really initiated was a long-term guarantee that would shoulder the auto industry with unaffordable retirement bills. Few businesses or unions seemed willing or able to calculate the impact of their pension deals. Drucker recounts that GM executives were so deluded about retirement costs that they reassured dubious directors that pensions would be fully paid from profits on investments in buoyant postwar stock markets.[3] GM's executives were the first of a long line of executives who punted to future generations the burden of making good on pension promises.

The pensions GM approved in 1950 were defined benefit plans, which commit employers to paying workers fixed pensions at a fixed retirement date. Embedded in collective bargaining negotiations, the benefit became a contractual right that companies could no longer terminate or shrink at their discretion. As each round of contract talks arrived, the ever-present threat of strikes in the booming manufacturing sector gave the union leverage to demand richer retirement benefits. By the early 1970s, U.S. auto worker pensions had more than tripled in value and included cost-of-living allowances and drug and healthcare benefits. These golden benefits began to migrate to Canada's private sector in the 1950s, after the UAW was able to negotiate pension benefits for the first time in contract talks with Ford Motor Co. workers in Windsor.[4]

Defined benefits were also prolific for federal, provincial, and municipal employees. Governments embraced the sturdy plans as an inducement for public sector jobs that could not compete with private sector wages. Government pensions like those first granted to Loyalist soldiers and Ontario teachers are rooted in a tradition of paying public workers for service to their country. By the 1970s, the vast majority of federal, provincial, and municipal employees were covered by fixed defined benefits, many of which came with expensive perks such as cost-of-living allowances and early retirement rights, some of which were available through unclaimed sick days. The financial health of these government plans was dependent on the investment prowess and integrity of the trustees, directors, and politicians who oversaw the funds. These qualities varied sharply from one pension plan to another. For many politicians, the long-term viability of pension funds took a backseat to taxpayer pressure to keep current budgets under control.

Some governments viewed pension fund savings as a captive money market. The Canada Pension Plan (CPP), the mandatory federal pension savings scheme founded in 1966, conveniently invested most of its assets in federal and provincial debt during its early life. The Ontario government seldom had to worry about finding buyers for its debt securities because its largest pension plan, the Ontario Teachers' Superannuation Fund (a precursor to the Ontario Teachers' Pension Plan), was restricted to buying provincial debentures. Retirement savings of Ontario teachers built the province's roads, bridges, and hospitals. The problem with the scheme was that the province got to decide what interest rate it would pay when it sold debentures to the pension plan (the rate could not be less than the average rate Ontario paid on long-term bonds sold in the previous year). When double-digit inflation sent interest rates soaring in the 1980s, teachers began to complain they were earning below-market returns on their pension savings. The debentures were so cloaked in secrecy that one commissioner overseeing the teachers' plan was blocked when he demanded to examine the securities in a Queen's Park vault.[5] The lack of transparency prompted some plan members to refer to the securities as "phantom debentures" or "fairy money." Political pressure from Ontario teachers and other pension advocates led to reforms in the 1990s that severed government control over investments. Ontario Teachers' and later CPP were freed to diversify their investments, policies that saw both funds more than quadruple their assets under administration to more than $300 billion as of 2013.

Canada's modern pension system has come a long way since Loyalist soldiers were granted meagre pensions in the early 1880s. Today, it is a highly evolved structure with three pillars of government, workplace, and personal saving pension programs. It is designed to protect vulnerable elderly from poverty and to foster government, workplace, and personal retirement savings plans that can replace a significant share of employees' incomes in their final years. In the buoyant postwar years, it seemed this promise was within reach as government benefits for the elderly grew, workplace pension benefits improved, plan membership expanded, and tax-friendly personal retirement savings plans were introduced.

By the late 1990s and throughout the 2000s, however, the pension vision began to disintegrate. There were many causes. Workers began to live much longer during retirement than anyone had predicted, baby boom workers began to retire, and plunging rates of return on traditional bonds and other fixed interest investments pushed pension funds into the riskier stock market investments. These fault lines were exposed by the dot-com crash in 2002 and the financial crisis of 2008. Just as the aging population was putting increased strains on pension plans, market failures pushed the solvency ratios of funds to all-time lows. Pension plans were never designed to withstand these threats.

Like many countries, Canada has three pension pillars. The first is federally funded benefits, Old Age Security (OAS), and the Guaranteed Income Supplement (GIS), modest monthly payments introduced in the 1970s largely to assist seniors with little or no income. This pension tier has been so successful that Canada now enjoys one of the world's lowest senior poverty rates in the world. The second pillar is government-sponsored workplace pensions that are funded with contributions from employers, employees, and the self-employed. The Canada Pension Plan covers all workers except those in Quebec, which has the Quebec Pension Plan. These plans pay a base pension that is roughly equal to about 25 per cent of an employee's salary up to a maximum of $12,150 as of 2013. The third pillar is Canada's most fragile. It consists of workplace pension plans and tax-deductible savings accounts known as registered retirement savings plans (RRSPs).

In the golden postwar years, corporate-, union-, and government-sponsored workplace pension plans (the third pillar) were so prolific that nearly 50 per cent of Canadian workers were plan members. The vast majority were defined benefit plans that required workers and their employers to make regular contributions to pensions that would pay fixed incomes and benefits at a set retirement date. These retirement savings plans were so effective that workers could look forward with certainty to a retirement income that typically replaced 60 per cent to 70 per cent of salaries.

The advantage of defined benefit plans is that employee savings are pooled into a large fund that can afford professional investment managers, charge smaller management fees, invest in diverse assets, and divide the risks of investment losses and increased retiree longevity among a broad membership.

These secure pension benefits are affordable as long as workers significantly outnumbered retirees and the plan earned adequate investment returns. If the ratio of workers to retirees shrinks, younger workers or their employers have to assume the burden of paying larger contributions to compensate for any investment losses and unexpected increases in the lifespan of retirees. The other essential pension equation is that the average worker's career is supposed to be significantly longer than his or her retirement years, allowing plenty of time to save for life after work. In the 1970s, for example, employees were living on average only seven years after retirement.

Investment gains were so consistent at many of Canada's large defined benefit plans that for years these returns masked the strains of an aging workforce. The first signs of trouble appeared in the late 1980s in the manufacturing and natural resources sectors, which historically sponsored the largest share of Canada's private sector pension plans. Auto, steel, and other manufacturers, and the natural resources companies that supplied these industries, began losing market share to more efficient global competitors. When one-time business giants, such as Toronto-based agriculture equipment maker Massey Combines Corp., tumbled into bankruptcy in the late 1980s, some of its biggest debts were pension plan deficits. Massey's failure marked one of the first times that thousands of Canadian workers and retirees were stranded with reduced pensions. In the years to come, even bigger Canadian businesses would fail, delivering to employees the harsh lesson that they could no longer take their pension guarantees for granted. As companies found themselves in bankruptcy court, pensioners learned that the "guarantees" were worthless.

Another challenge is falling mortality rates. Retirees are dying at significantly slower rates, which means, to put it bluntly, there is not enough turnover. Today, Canadians are living decades beyond their retirement. Most employers didn't anticipate the huge shift because life expectancy scholars turned out to be poor forecasters. From 1929 to 2000, life expectancy experts saw their published forecasts routinely shattered. Pioneering U.S. demographic statistician Louis Dublin concluded in 1928 that life expectancy would peak at about sixty-five years.[6] What he was unable to account for were huge medical breakthroughs, such as antibiotics, that would dramatically extend lifespans. Since the 1920s, lifespans in affluent nations have grown from sixty-five years to nearly eighty. In Canada, men are currently expected to live until seventy-nine, women to eighty-four. If longevity rates continue at this pace, life expectancy will reach one hundred in sixty years.

We are getting there quickly. Canadians who have lived a century are the fastest-growing segment of the population. The 2011 census counted 5,800 centenarians, a number that is on track to grow to 78,300 by 2061.[7] That is enough hundred-year-olds to match the population of Sault Ste. Marie. These remarkable lifespans are stretching the resources of pension plans that were never designed to support so many elderly members. In the not too distant future, the average retiree will spend more time collecting their pensions than they did contributing to them during their careers. Our pension designers never anticipated this trend.

Over the next twenty years, more than 7 million Canadian workers will retire. Baby boomers, the forty-five- to sixty-five-year-old workers who account for 42 per cent of the country's workforce, will join the largest job exodus in Canadian history. Replacing them will be a smaller pool of younger workers in Canada's shrinking workforce. This imbalance is eroding some pension plan models that were built on the assumption that young workers would always outnumber retirees. Twenty years from now, it is estimated there will be two workers or less for every retiree. For the Ontario Teachers' Pension Plan, which oversees one of the country's largest and oldest pension memberships, the shift is even more dramatic. Today there are only 1.5 active workers for every retired teacher. That ratio is expected to continue shrinking as more teachers, some of Canada's healthiest employees, head out the door for a retirement that is projected to last for more than thirty years.

Some pension plan sponsors have adjusted to spiralling pension costs by pushing into new investment frontiers. For many years pension funds generated enough investment gains to pay for pension obligations by simply buying bonds and other fixed-rate investments. In the 1950s, plan managers concluded that they could increase portfolio returns by investing significant amounts into higher yielding stocks. The strategy was a pension elixir – boosting returns, lowering costs, and financing more generous benefits. What managers ignored, however, was that bigger stock market bets brought increased investment risks. Actuaries, who are tasked with evaluating pension health, compounded the problem by allowing plan sponsors to apply more optimistic investment return projections, or discount rates, to estimate how much they could earn to pay future pension bills. This widespread practice meant pension funds were not building sufficient reserves to weather market storms. As interest rates started to decline in the 1990s, the funds further diversified into so-called alternative investments such as real estate, commodities, infrastructure projects, private equity, and hedge funds to keep up with the bills. During the booming late 1990s and early 2000s, this strategy delivered a bounty of investment profits. But the tide went out after the double whammy of the 2001 dot-com crash and 2008 financial crisis. Five months after the market meltdown in September 2008, the typical pension plan in Canada lost about 20 per cent of its asset value. The aggregate funding shortfall of defined benefit pension plans was a staggering $350 billion, an amount equal to the gross domestic product (GDP) of Quebec.[8] Pensions that boasted surpluses for years were saddled with shortfalls just as the first wave of baby boomers were retiring. Many had years to replenish these deficits; others simply ran out of time. The financial crisis pushed a number of major employers with pension shortfalls into bankruptcy proceedings. Their plight left workers and retirees with reduced pensions.

In Canada, some municipal pension deficits ballooned so dramatically that they exceeded annual revenues, forcing hiring freezes and the suspension of some local services. Pension failures were even more devastating in the United States. Pension debts pushed two U.S. cities, Vallejo, California, and Central Falls, Rhode Island, into bankruptcy and was a key factor in the recent filing by Detroit, Michigan. Another troubled town, Prichard, Alabama, simply stopped sending cheques to its 154 retired employees. These are not isolated cases. Even with overly optimistic investment and mortality estimates, U.S. state-run pension plans are more than $1 trillion short of the assets needed to pay their pension obligations. Several experts argue the deficit is significantly higher because the plans are not using realistic discount rates to gauge the assets needed to pay the pension bills.

Many employers have responded to the growing burden by terminating or shrinking the pension benefit. Since 1977, the percentage of Canadian employees covered by workplace pension plans has fallen to 39 per cent from 46 per cent of the workforce. Most of the decline was driven by the private sector, which by 2010 was only offering pensions to a quarter of all employees.[9] Public sector workers have fared much better, with more than 95 per cent of employees still covered by reliable defined benefit pensions. In the private sector, fixed defined benefit pensions are a dying breed, with only 12 per cent of employees belonging to defined benefit plans as of 2010.

Many businesses have replaced these pension commitments with a riskier benefit known as defined contribution plans. These retirement programs, which are typically voluntary, call for employees, and in some cases employers, to contribute fixed payments to pension savings. Unlike defined benefits, which promise a fixed retirement income for life on a fixed date, the value of defined contribution pensions fluctuates with market swings. Employees must wait until retirement to open their pension box to learn the value of their savings and what level of income their pension savings will provide, which is largely shaped by prevailing interest rates on that date. Adding to the uncertainty is longevity. Have employees saved enough for a retirement that may last longer than expected? Another big disadvantage of defined contribution plans is that pension savings are divided into individual accounts that burden employees with the cost of expensive investment management fees. This highly fragmented pension system is a huge disadvantage for workers because management fees are significantly larger than those paid by larger defined benefit funds that have the scale to hire in-house investment professionals at a lower overall management cost.

As it turns out, stressed defined benefit and defined contribution pension members are Canada's lucky employees. More than 60 per cent of Canadian workers do not even belong to a workplace pension. Most will rely on a combination of personal savings, the Canada Pension Plan, and federal OAS and GIS supplements. For many retirees, personal savings won't be much help. In recent years, Canadian consumers have only set aside a threadbare 5.5 per cent of their income, a sharp drop from a 20 per cent savings rate in the 1980s.

RRSPs were introduced with great fanfare in the 1950s to help fill the pension gap. The plans were designed to induce Canadians to save with tax-friendly terms that allowed investments in RRSPs to be deducted from incomes. But most RRSP holders are novices when it comes to making investment choices. Making matters worse, management fees on individual RRSP accounts are so costly that investment gains have largely been neutered. Another big disadvantage is longevity risk. Unlike defined benefit pensions, where members collectively share the risk that some retirees will live longer than others, RRSP holders and defined contribution plan members are on their own. Without knowing how long they will live after retirement, these investors will have to save significantly more to ensure they have enough to cover uncertain retirement lifespans. Canadian workers have such meagre retirement savings plans that an estimated 30 per cent of modest to high-income households will experience a significant drop in their standard of living in retirement.[10] This will be a painful adjustment for retirees and an enormous blow to the industries and services that rely on their business.

The shrinking nest egg will put an increased burden on the federal government and taxpayers, which already spend $36 billion annually on OAS, GIS, and related spousal payments, the largest single federal expense ahead of healthcare and defence. This burden is expected to triple by 2030, a staggering cost that could grow even bigger if the erosion in workplace pensions continues. A country that is admired around the globe for nearly eliminating geriatric poverty is potentially facing a new century of retirement hardship with a pension system that is in danger of becoming as worn out as Canada's first pensioners.

It doesn't have to end this way. Pension reforms in other jurisdictions, including some Canadian provinces, have been available for years. But instead of debating what options can best work for the country, our business, labour, and political leaders are preoccupied with laying blame or denying the enormity of the looming crisis. Businesses will say unions are to blame for the pension meltdown because they demanded excessively rich retirement terms. Unions retort that companies have so poorly managed their businesses or employee pension funds that they are reneging on their contracts. Politicians, loath to go near the third rail, reassure us our pension fears are overstated. Others, like those in the city of Saint John, would rather fight pension critics in court than confront the awful truth of unsustainable pensions. Ottawa's current solution to the mess is to promote a new savings product, pooled registered pension plans (PRPP), for employees or self-employed individuals without pensions. The plan seeks to lower pension costs by pooling individual contributions in a large fund, but critics argue the approach will have limited success because enrolment is voluntary.

Rarely does the pension argument acknowledge the root cause of the retirement meltdown: record numbers of workers are retiring and living longer than anyone anticipated; pension funds have not built in sufficient surpluses to cope with market and demographic stresses; and, employers are increasingly unable or unwilling to shoulder ballooning pension costs. While the system deteriorates, the gap between those with pensions and those with insufficient retirement plans grows, and instead of a productive exchange of reform ideas, there is a tug-of-war between these two groups. This debate is dividing the very people who must come to the table to start the tough process of building a new and affordable model.

In Canada, the pension discord has become so furious that some target workers with defined benefit pension plans that actually provide an affordable social safety net for our aging population. Rather than focusing their efforts on reforming these plans to ensure long-term sustainability, some politicians want to further weaken the system by shredding what is left of effective workplace pensions. They target public sector employees, many of whom have invested a substantial share of their paycheques in defined benefit plans. In this debate, the rallying cry is: why should taxpayers foot the bill for civil service pensions that the majority of taxpayers don't have? While there is certainly room to reform public sector pensions, this so-called solution is not a money saver for taxpayers. In fact, this teardown of existing defined benefit plans will ultimately hand a bigger financial burden to Canadian taxpayers.

Today, 6 million Canadians belong to registered pension plans, of which 3.1 million are employed in the public sector. The vast majority of government workers have defined benefit plans. Canada's top ten government-sponsored plans have accumulated more than $700 billion in assets. From 1996 to 2011, public sector funds in Canada generated annual investment returns of 7 per cent, compared with 5 per cent in private sector funds.[11] As a result of these profits, most major funds pay about two-thirds of their members' pensions from investment income; the balance comes from employee and employer contributions. If the public sector follows the private sector and replaces defined benefit plans with riskier defined contributions, large, efficient pools of pension savings will be divided into small, individual plans that could never match their investment successes or clout.

In such a scenario, Canada will witness the erosion of some of its biggest pension funds and one of the country's largest capital pools. It will also pass on to future generations of taxpayers the burden of supporting millions of additional workers who would lose secure pensions. If public sector defined benefit pensions were terminated today, Canadian taxpayers would be facing a bigger bill down the road. Today, only 20 per cent of 3.4 million defined benefit pension members in Canada are eligible to receive federal GIS supplements, nearly half the 37 per cent participation rate by other retirees not covered by defined benefit pensions.[12] The federal government's GIS bill would inevitably increase without the safety net of sustainable defined benefit plans.

It is time to stop wasting our energy on blame. It is time to look for solutions. The longer we wait, the more difficult the inevitable reforms. This is no longer an imaginary scenario: pension failures have pushed U.S. companies and municipalities into bankruptcies, stranded some retirees with virtually nothing, and threatened the solvency of at least one of Canada's weakest provinces. Workers and retirees have made sacrifices, some of them at great personal cost, to redesign pensions that were no longer viable.

Our book offers three case studies of pension reform in jurisdictions with retirement systems in various stages of disrepair. One was imploding, the other inching near the cliff, and the third, ranked as one of the most admired pension systems in the world, was in duress. What these tales of reform share are political or labour leaders who had the courage to touch the third rail. They confronted damaged pension systems and won labour or political support for new models. The traditional defined benefit promise of a fully guaranteed fixed pension is rapidly fading in these regimes. Taking its place is a new shared-risk pension that places a priority on robust plans with sufficient surpluses to weather market and demographic swings. When these surpluses are endangered, workers and employers can choose between adding more savings to the pension pot, or downsizing retirement benefits to ensure their plans for long-term viability.

In New Brunswick, a Conservative premier collaborated with union leaders to overhaul dangerously underfunded pension plans. In Rhode Island, an elected Democratic treasurer stared down opposing unions to slay the pension dragon. Both regimes have created a new model that imposes strict funding rules and embeds new levers that hand pension plan managers the flexibility to adjust benefits in the face of economic and demographic threats.

In the Netherlands, pensions have been under constant construction since the early 2000s, when the country realized its pension promises had to be recalibrated to cope with financial shocks and longevity increases. The debate about a new pension model is still underway, but early moves toward more flexible hybrid plans left the world's richest pension system in much better shape to withstand financial storms. New Brunswick, Rhode Island, and the Netherlands are still navigating their fragile reforms through harsh political and legal headwinds, but they represent the beginnings of long-overdue resolve by political and labour leaders to fix crumbling pension systems. We can learn from their experiences as we address the task of reforming Canada's pension system.

CHAPTER 2

NEW BRUNSWICK

Palliative Care

When Samuel de Champlain discovered a snug harbour along the northeast coast of the Americas in 1604, he named it Saint John after the beheaded saint, John the Baptist. Like its namesake, Saint John and what became New Brunswick forged its identity through adversity. For almost two centuries after Champlain, Saint John was the object of raids and sieges as England and France battled to control the strategic port. Then late in the eighteenth century more visitors arrived: thousands of British Loyalists fleeing persecution after the American Revolution.

Britain's decision in 1784 to create New Brunswick as a haven for loyal refugees opened the floodgates for more than fourteen thousand Loyalists to descend on Saint John, then a tiny community of three thousand. The frontier town was so desolate that one arriving refugee, Sarah Frost, wrote, "It is, I think the roughest land I have ever seen."[1] Most Loyalists endured their first maritime winter in tents covered with spruce bows, battling snow and disease. The early hardships fostered a deep spirit of community that would carry the province through subsequent dark hours.

Fortunes changed when Britain turned to the colony in the Napoleonic Wars for shipbuilding timber. A "wood, wind and sail economy" kept the territory afloat until the late 1880s when iron-hulled steamships conquered the seas, sinking New Brunswick's core industry. Since then, the booms and busts of the province's forest, wood products, and mining sectors have continued to buffet New Brunswick's economy. Dependency on natural resources meant the province was hit hard during commodity slumps in the 1970s and 1980s. A job drought forced so many young workers to leave for work that New Brunswick's population shrank.

The outmigration also cut short the province's "echo boom" – children of baby boomers. This demographic hole leaves New Brunswick with an inordinate percentage of older workers and senior citizens. Nearly 20 per cent of the province's seven hundred and fifty thousand residents are over sixty-five. By 2030, non-workers will outnumber workers, an imbalance that means New Brunswick's vulnerable resources economy will be beset by pension breakdowns before the rest of Canada. Soon, the province's pension funds will have fewer active workers than retirees. Which is another way of saying that New Brunswick is ground zero in Canada's pension contagion.

New Brunswick received its first pension shock in 2004 when St. Anne-Nackawic Pulp Co. Ltd. declared bankruptcy, throwing four hundred people out of work. It was a devastating blow to the one-industry town near the Quebec border. Nackawic's one thousand residents relied so heavily on the pulp mill that in 1991 the community built a tribute to forestry – a five-storey statue that is the world's largest axe. Two months after the plant closure, another axe came down on local citizens when bankruptcy documents revealed the company's pension plan was so underfunded it could not pay promised pensions.

Only six years before the St. Anne pulp mill filed for bankruptcy, its two pension funds were financially robust, with a large surplus of assets. Between 1999 and

2002 the mill began compromising the pension by offering employees incentives to retire early. Instead of draining company payroll, early retirees would be paid by the pension fund. Soon, the company was writing so many pension cheques that actuarial advisers urged management to prop up underfunded plans. The company ignored the advice, and when it filed for bankruptcy in 2004, documents revealed a combined $40 million shortfall, meaning it had only 65 per cent of the assets needed to meet pension obligations.

More bad news followed. Provincial pension laws at the time gave retirees more rights than workers. Retirees' pensions had to be honoured at the expense of active workers, creating a toxic caste system. There was enough money left in pension funds to ensure the mill's two hundred and fifty retirees and workers over fifty-five would receive 85 per cent of their pensions. Almost nothing was left, however, for the two hundred and seventy-five laid-off workers who were under fifty-five, though many had made regular pension contributions for decades.

The harsh calculus divided a tightly knit community. Younger Peters were robbed to pay off older Pauls. Not surprisingly, legal and political battles were launched to challenge the decision. Still, bad blood boiled. Vera Hawkes, whose fifty-three-year-old husband was two years short of the mill's pension cut off age, told the

National Post: "We lost more than a pension and a job. People just don't care about each other as much."[2]

A disturbing report by New Brunswick ombudsman Bernard Richard on the harsh personal impact of the lost St. Anne pensions prompted the province to amend its pension act in December 2005.[3] The new laws effectively abolished discriminatory pension payout rules and forced the mill's older retirees to give up one-third of their pensions so that younger workers could preserve some of their retirement savings.

The mill reopened in 2006 under new owners who are shipping pulp to markets in East Asia. A few hundred jobs were restored, allowing some locals to start rebuilding shattered nest eggs. As for the hundreds of unemployed workers and retirees left on the sidelines, their shrunken pensions remain unchanged. Their plight is a cautionary tale to the rest of the province: pensions will never again be seen as a guarantee but as a promise that could be so badly broken that communities might be torn apart and younger workers left bearing the brunt of pension failures.

Four years after Nackawic, New Brunswick's pension disorder grew worse again. In 2009, U.S.–owned Fraser Paper Inc. filed for bankruptcy protection, revealing a $171 million deficit on five pension plans for workers in New Brunswick, Quebec, and the United States. The company was broken up and sold to creditors. In bankruptcy proceedings, pensions rank behind most other creditors, which in the Fraser case meant there was little left to replenish drained pension funds. The U.S. government's pension guarantee funds covered the losses of its citizens, but Fraser's New Brunswick workers were left without a safety net. About eight hundred retirees saw pensions slashed by 30 to 40 per cent.

Scores of other New Brunswick pension funds were also rocked by the global 2008 financial crisis, which sent asset values plummeting. Across Canada, the value of corporate and government investment holdings crashed, leaving many without assets to pay existing and future pensions. Careless pension management and a frail economy made matters worse in New Brunswick. Local pension plans relied on outdated forecast models that underestimated retiree lifespan while overstating future investment returns. Some had no surpluses for rainy days because employers took contribution holidays. Some unions allowed surpluses to be diverted to pay for enhanced pension benefits. Simply put, workers and employers hadn't saved enough. Elsewhere, Canadian pension funds had decades to replenish damaged plans before being hit by baby boom retirements; New Brunswick had less financial muscle and time to fix pension promises that were based on faulty assumptions.

Among the hardest hit New Brunswick pensions was a plan for ten thousand working and retired nurses and healthcare and community employees. Healthcare employees enjoy great benefits because of incentives needed to draw workers to an aging, sparsely settled province. New Brunswick nurses earned average salaries of $72,000, while making a modest pension contribution equal to 5.25 per cent of their paycheques – one of the lowest rates in the province. Further weakening the plan, the provincial government, which employs nurses and healthcare workers, had been allowed to spend the fund's surplus to enhance pension benefits. The practice, unchallenged by union and plan members, left the fund with little cushion to absorb market shocks.

When the 2008 financial crisis struck, the pension fund was mortally wounded. By the end of 2008, the value of assets plunged to $830 million from $1.2 billion, leaving the plan with a deficit in excess of $340 million.[4] It was a brutal blow for a fund facing a huge increase in retirements. In the nurses union, more than 40 per cent of workers are over fifty-five, leaving little time to recoup the losses.

The crisis left a pension committee of union and provincial government representatives with few options. The first: ask the province for money to restock depleted funds. But after months of little response from the Liberal government of Premier Shawn Graham, the plan's two unions – the New Brunswick Nurses Union and the New Brunswick Union of Public Employees Association – took action. On June 26, 2009, the plan's governing committee met inside the squat, red brick Wu Conference Centre at the University of New Brunswick. Gathering in the Fredericton campus at a large horseshoe table were the unions' senior executives and a handful of provincial officials. Joining them were two advisers who would become indispensable pension paramedics.

In his mid-forties, Conrad Ferguson is tall and rangy, with a thick crop of grey-flecked black hair. He looks more like an outdoorsman than an actuary who has devoted a career to studying statistics and running computer models to advise pension funds. His gravelly voice, quiet demeanour, and uncanny ability to forecast the implications of pension modifications would frequently be put to good use as New Brunswick struggled to fix its pension system.

Sue Rowland, an outspoken lawyer in her mid-sixties, followed an unlikely career path to pensions. After hopping from teaching, secretarial work, and TV journalism in Toronto, she said during an interview for this book that she settled on law because "I was tired of influencing people. I wanted the legal power to force change." Rowland spent years working as a lawyer with the Government of Ontario, defending workers in labour disputes. She became entranced with pension law after appearing in a Toronto court in 1988 on the day Massey Combines Corp. filed for bankruptcy protection with a pension deficit. Rowland represented Ontario's pension benefit guarantee fund. While lawyers and creditors jockeyed for the judge's attention that day, an elderly man raised his hand, approached the bench, and nervously asked if he was losing his pension. Spying Rowland, the judge gently directed the pensioner her way. With Rowland's help, the man joined three thousand Massey retirees who would receive pensions of up to $1,000 a month from the province to make up for Massey's shortfall. The case hooked Rowland on pension law, which was rapidly becoming a battleground between failing companies, creditors, and employees. "I am a rescuer, and I saw a huge need for employees in these cases," she said.

Rowland has represented governments or workers in some of the country's biggest corporate restructurings, including Algoma Steel and the Canadian arms of Chrysler and General Motors. By the late 2000s, job stress had taken a toll on her health. She selected less demanding cases and devoted time to her octogenarian husband. One 2004 assignment she did accept was advising New Brunswick medical workers. Rowland initially hoped to travel to the province a few times a year, but she and her husband were so attracted to the friendly, no-nonsense Maritimes that they bought a second home near Fredericton. She delights in shocking the province's staid pension and business fraternity. "I freaked everyone out," she said with a deep laugh. The property she purchased once belonged to the small city's notorious madam and bootlegger, One-Eyed Pat. "I like to tell people the difference between me and One-Eyed Pat is that she made her money at night and I make mine during the day." By 2011, Rowland would be working many nights in New Brunswick. At a June meeting, Ferguson had a chilling message for the unions and Rowland: if the pension plan were wound up at that moment, the actuary declared it would be 35 per cent short of the assets needed to pay existing obligations. With no imminent funding help from the province, he said, the plan had some tough decisions. Employees would have to increase pension contributions by an additional 8.55 per cent of salary or the value of future benefits would be reduced by 66 per cent. Both options put an enormous burden on current workers. Without drastic measures, the actuary warned, the pension plan was no longer sustainable. "It was the holy shit moment," said Rowland. "That's when we knew it was going in the tank. Unsustainable is actuarial code for bankruptcy."

New Brunswick premier David Alward was making his way through another packed working day in late March 2011 when he took time to visit with his pension consultants. Six months earlier, his Conservative Party had been elected to office after Shawn Graham's Liberals had been voted out by a tide of opposition to a plan to sell the province's hydro utility. An earnest, down-to-earth, former agriculture minister, Alward won voters with promises to freeze power rates, lower provincial debt, and improve medical care. He also committed to bolster pension protections. Son of a Baptist reverend, he had been raised in Nackawic and was horrified by the suffering inflicted on close friends who had seen pension plans shredded.

Alward's appointment that afternoon was with two of three people his government had hired four months earlier to study the long-term stability of private sector pensions. He had given the task force wide berth to investigate pensions sponsored by New Brunswick businesses and governments. He did not want to be caught unprepared for the next Nackawic or Fraser Paper. If other pensions were foundering, Alward wanted them fixed before it was too late.

Waiting for him in a small meeting room near his office in Fredericton's grey stone and glass Centennial Building were a handful of senior cabinet ministers and their deputies. Joining them was lawyer Sue Rowland and Paul McCrossan, a retired actuary and former federal Conservative Member of Parliament (MP) from Scarborough, Ontario. Rowland's progress with the local nurses and hospital workers pension plan had brought her to Alward's attention. She agreed to join the province's pension task force on one condition: she would not sign up without McCrossan, whose reputation for sniffing out risks was the stuff of legend in actuarial circles.

A Conservative MP in the late 1970s and 1980s, McCrossan once introduced a private member's bill tightening rules for federal pension reporting. A former actuary with Canada Life Insurance, McCrossan was troubled by Ottawa's spotty public disclosure of pension costs. After probing, he uncovered a whopper cover-up that Canada's Auditor General would in 1982 describe as a $12.5 billion "omission." The Trudeau government had overstated its fiscal performance for years by neglecting to report the multibillion-dollar costs of adjusting federal civil service pension payments for inflation increases.[5] McCrossan's bill ensured pension costs could never again be concealed.

After politics, McCrossan rose to prominence in actuarial circles as the president of the Canadian Institute of Actuaries and the new International Actuarial Association. He was later appointed to the Standards Advisory Council of the International Accounting Standards Board. He studied Dutch pension reforms for Canadian clients and served on Britain's Morris Review of the actuarial profession that analyzed pension reform. Nearly seventy when Rowland called him, McCrossan accepted the New Brunswick post assuming it would be a short-term contract. Rounding out the task force was Pierre-Marcel Desjardins, a regional economist with the University of Moncton who was unable to attend the March session.

Alward entered the meeting hoping the task force would help guide the province to a less expensive pension system. Only 30 per cent of New Brunswick's workers had pensions and the majority of these were expensive, defined benefit plans, committing employers to pay fixed pensions to retirees. The costly plans, coupled with widespread fund deficits and a weak economy, put a burden on government and business. Many Canadian employers had recently moved to what appeared to be less costly defined contribution plans, shifting risks to employees. Such plans only required employers to contribute fixed amounts to pension savings, leaving the final value of pensions subject to market whims. A number of New Brunswick's biggest employers, including the Irving family, offered employees defined contribution plans. If defined contribution plans were good enough for the Irvings, Alward and some key cabinet members believed, they were good enough for the rest of the province.

The defined contribution discussion would be short. The health of New Brunswick's pension system, Rowland and McCrossan explained, was worse than the task force had feared. Almost all private sector pension funds had sizeable deficits. Of the three hundred pension plans registered in the province, only three were fully funded. New Brunswick's cities and municipalities were also struggling with large pension deficits. Four years after the pension board of the city of Saint John had sued councillor John Ferguson for libel, the $45 million pension deficit had ballooned to $130 million, a staggering bill that nearly matched the city's total 2011 revenues of $138 million.

Widespread pension deficits, McCrossan explained, were not only due to the 2008 financial crisis. Lax pension management was a problem. Many funds were receiving insufficient contributions from employees and employers to weather market and longevity shocks. New Brunswick's pension funds were seriously ill at the worst possible time. In a few years, the rising tide of baby boom retirements would strand a province already suffering a shortage of younger workers with insufficient pension savings. "The demographics are going to eat you alive," McCrossan recalled telling the premier.

Alward went pale as he absorbed the news. You did not need to be an actuary to understand the gravity of the situation. New Brunswick's pension system might soon implode. Converting to defined contribution plans was not going to fix this problem; in fact, it would make things worse. When defined benefit pension plans are wound up, employers are required to account for the funding shortfall immediately, a burden that could add untold billions of dollars to the provincial deficit. If the province did nothing, it was not inconceivable that municipalities such as Saint John could be forced into bankruptcy proceedings, hoisting the burden of paying pension benefits onto the province. The crisis had been building for years, but for too long, New Brunswick's political, corporate, and union leadership were unwilling or unable to address the festering problem. Staring into the abyss, Alward said he realized the situation had become so grave that "we couldn't afford any longer to punt it."

McCrossan and Rowland reassured the premier that it was possible to avert the crisis if he was prepared to reinvent how pensions were structured and regulated. Alward listened quietly for most of the two-and-a-half-hour session. Near the end he asked consultants a question he would repeat frequently when he met with the task force:

"What is the right thing to do?"

Rowland fired off a tart response: "Do you want a shelf improvement kit?" she said in reference to countless government studies and task force reports that gather dust on shelves of forgotten closets. "Or do you want to fix this?" She continued, "Because this can be fixed, you just have to give us time."

Alward glanced at the unlikely pension fixers – a greying, left-leaning labour lawyer and a retired actuary and former Conservative Party MP. They really believed they could find a way to work with fractious municipal politicians, stubborn unions, and hard-pressed employers to reform a broken pension system? It was an impossible mission, but at the moment, New Brunswick had few other options.

"Fix it," the premier ordered.

Rowland and McCrossan walked away surprised. They had both wasted a lot of time unsuccessfully lobbying Ontario and federal politicians of all stripes to bolster pension protections. They had seen the storm clouds for years. Alward was the first party leader who actually was prepared to tackle the politically fraught job of telling workers, unions, and employers that sacrifices were needed to save their teetering pensions.

"He wasn't looking for a way to spin it, he really was committed to fixing it," Rowland said. For his part,

Alward was not feeling very courageous after listening to the consultants. "I felt sick to my stomach," he now says.

❦

The task force followed a simple strategy in hopes of pulling New Brunswick out of its pension hole: their first step was targeting the most seriously infected plans to ring-fence the contagion. If they could save the critically ill funds, they could avert a panic and spare local businesses, municipalities, and the province a crippling run of bankruptcies and bailouts. Early pension victories were essential to win over other dubious employers, unions, and workers. The more plans that fell into line, the easier it would be to win support for radical reforms.

Pierre-Marcel Desjardins, the Moncton University economist and third member of the task force, was horrified when he realized the seriousness of the pension crisis. He had devoted his career to studying the frail regional economy of New Brunswick. Its resources sector had been in the dumps for years; unemployment rates were among the highest in the country; companies were struggling to stay afloat. The added stress of pension deficits could result in disaster. "Pension plan members were calling me and telling me how dire the situation was," Desjardins recalled in an interview for this book.

"We were talking about peoples' livelihood. I realized if we didn't do anything we were going to fall off a cliff."

The toughest challenge was Saint John. The city shouldered one of the province's biggest pension deficits and managed the plan with outdated mortality tables and investment assumptions. Neither the city nor its workers had contributed enough to the maturing pension plan, which had almost as many retirees as workers. The disability pensions that incensed John Ferguson in 2005 were small potatoes. Bigger issues were the plan's aging workforce, heavy bets in the stock market, and overly optimistic projections about long-term profits on these investments. When the 2008 financial crisis hit, the fund was hammered. The situation was so bleak that Rowland would warn the city at a 2012 public council meeting that its pension "is the worst plan I have ever seen." Applying more realistic mortality and investment projections, she estimated the fund was actually facing a $342 million deficit, a funding hole that was nearly three times the city's annual revenues.

Rowland and McCrossan were assigned to come up with solutions for the gravely wounded plan. McCrossan believed the Saint John pension could be returned to health if all sides – the city, workers, even retirees – were prepared to make sacrifices. McCrossan learned from studying Dutch reforms in the 2000s that radical adjustments were attainable. He had also understood from his advisory work in Britain that there was a limit to how far pensioners could be pushed. Reforms introduced by the British government in 2010 were so harsh that a political backlash forced the government to abandon some initiatives. The task force would need to work closely with the city to calibrate the right mix of changes.

Working with Saint John, however, was no easy matter. The city's mayor, Ivan Court, favoured the traditional political strategy of delaying rather than fixing the problem. The 2007 libel suit launched by the city's pension board against councillor John Ferguson was crawling through the courts when the task force arrived in 2011. The first judge to review the case in 2007, Mr. Justice Hugh McLellan, dismissed the libel claims against Ferguson on the grounds that municipal politicians enjoy legal protections when making disparaging comments on public issues.[6] For decades, Canada's courts had given politicians wide berth to speak their minds to ensure free discussion. The city appealed McLellan's decision and won the right to a trial that would be fought over the issue of whether Ferguson was motivated by malice when allegedly defaming the board. That ruling unleashed a volley of pre-trial motions, hundreds of hours of pre-trial witness examinations, and more than one hundred thousand pages of court documents.

Local media had a field day with the libel case. A struggling city with Canada's highest unemployment rate and a troubled pension plan was spending millions in legal costs to sue an elected official.[7] Media websites were filled with comments from locals cheering Ferguson's David in his battle with Goliath city elders. Faced with bad publicity and a looming election, the city's political leadership did not appear eager to concede tough decisions should have been made years earlier to reduce pension deficits. Instead of reform, Mayor Court asked the provincial government for extra time to top up its pension. The city wanted twenty-five years, instead of the required fifteen, to pay off the deficit. "We're hoping that the cabinet will do the right thing. It doesn't cost them anything," Court told the CBC in January 2011.

Rowland had more success with the nurses and hospital workers pension plan. After their actuary, Conrad Ferguson, dispensed grim pension deficit news in 2009, a committee of union and government representatives endorsed a recommendation that benefit cuts be shared by all members, including retirees. In the shadow of Nackawic, sacrifices had to be equitable. The committee dispatched Ferguson and Rowland to find a fair, pragmatic solution. The committee's willingness to swallow harsh medicine was crucial. Few unions cede core benefits such as pensions without a fight. But the nursing and hospital employee union leaders on the committee understood from the beginning that they needed to move quickly to save their damaged plan. Maybe the swift, practical response was instinct – the response of medical workers who had spent careers devoted to helping families and patients navigate devastating diagnoses.

Marilyn Quinn was elected president of the New Brunswick Nurses Union in 2004 after twenty years as a palliative care nurse. Her placid optimism reassured the fund's workers and retirees. "You can't work in palliative care and not have hope," says Quinn of the years she spent helping families reconcile themselves to death. When she heard the pension diagnosis in 2009, she says, "I put on my palliative care glasses. It was time to be honest and tell people what they didn't want to hear."

Her counterpart, Susie Proulx-Daigle at the New Brunswick Union, had a tougher challenge. Her group was a local of Canadian Union of Public Employees, whose national leaders strongly oppose pension cuts. "I told them that we had our own problems in New Brunswick and that we were going to solve them our way. We are more of a social union. We are part of communities that work together to fix our problems."

To prepare members for harsh medicine, the unions made two crucial decisions. The first was trusting membership with bad news. Shortly after meeting with their actuary in June 2009, the unions alerted members in a newsletter that pension benefits could be reduced or changed and contributions increased to fortify the wounded fund. It was the beginning of a three-year campaign of notices, meetings, and a "let's talk" tour. "Transparency was essential; we told them what was happening and they trusted us to do the right thing," said Quinn.

The other decision was to follow Rowland's advice to seek direction from the courts regarding the pension committee's right to change plan benefits and contributions. After two days of hearings, Mr. Justice William Grant of the Court of Queen's Bench of New Brunswick handed down a decision on July 8, 2011, that would help pave the way to pension reform. Grant made three key findings. Recognizing the serious condition of the pension plan, he ruled that the governing committee of the Nurses and New Brunswick Union had a legal obligation to protect the long-term survival of the pension plan, even if that meant imposing benefit cuts. He ruled that the committee had the power to eliminate cost-of-living allowances (COLA) from the pensions of active workers. COLA increases, Justice Grant ruled, were not a benefit accrued during workers' careers but rather a perk earned on retirement day. The flip side of Grant's ruling was that retirees' COLAs could not be touched. Stripping a benefit that was already being paid to retirees would be a contractual violation. On the issue of asking workers to increase paycheque pension contributions, Grant ruled such hikes were possible, provided the employer, in this case the Government of New Brunswick, similarly increased its contributions to the plan.

Although the pension plan prevailed on only one of three requests, Rowland and her clients made significant legal headway. Grant's decision marked one of the few times a Canadian court allowed a solvent pension plan to change benefits without a membership vote or collective bargaining process. The struggling pension fund had a green light to suspend a perk it could no longer afford.

Grant's decision also sharpened the legal boundaries of pension rights. If troubled funds needed to scale back payments to retirees or ask employees and employers to save more for pensions, New Brunswick had to change its laws. Alward was willing, but before he introduced laws to shrink pension benefits, he had to ensure his government was bulletproof. That meant rolling back rich pensions for provincial politicians. Members of the Legislative Assembly (MLAs) in New Brunswick had won the pension jackpot in 2008 when the Graham government approved a payroll change that stapled tax-free expense allowances onto their base salaries. The switch did not put any new money into MLAs' pockets but doubled the base from which pension benefits were calculated. MLAs with ten years of service saw their pensions rise to $38,000 from $16,325. In the wake of Nackawic, the pension windfall was a political powder keg. Alward's election campaign in 2010 included a promise to revisit the lucrative retirement benefits, and in the summer of 2011 he announced a plan to erase most of the pension gains. Ten-year pensions would be rolled back to $20,400. MLAs would be the province's first pension beneficiaries, outside of bankruptcy proceedings, to swallow significant benefit reductions. "It was the right thing to do. We needed to be part of the change," Alward said.

For the next ten months the task force and Alward's government worked behind the scenes to draft new legislation and calculate the right mix of pension cuts and funding increases needed to rescue their retirement system. Although reformers were confident they could find financial solutions, they were uncertain of political support. "We were taking a significant risk as a government," Alward said. About 70 per cent of the province's workers did not have pensions. If the government was too generous with troubled funds, which largely covered public sector workers, it could have a taxpayer rebellion. He had to convince unions and voters that a pension overhaul would save the province from a financial meltdown.

The best insurance against political failure, he believed, was winning union support. Labour leaders are not in the habit of collaborating with Conservative governments, but the province had an influential labour adviser on its task force. Rowland had been impressed with Alward's commitment to reform. "I've never met a politician like him before," she said. "He means what he says. He was serious about fixing the pensions."

The government's other advantage was Rowland's clients. The nurses and hospital workers unions were already focused on cuts to save their endangered plan. After Justice Grant's decision, Rowland encouraged unions to meet with Alward in late 2011 to pave the way for a new approach. Alward promised union chiefs Quinn and Proulx-Daigle that he would support a collaborative approach. If they worked with the task force to repair broken pension funds, their solution could be a template for other ailing funds. The unions agreed to discuss rescue plans with Rowland, McCrossan, and Desjardins. The early sessions were so confrontational, however, that collaboration seemed unlikely. In one of their first meetings, McCrossan advised Quinn and Proulx-Daigle that their members would have to shoulder significant benefit cuts. Pensions would have to be calculated from lower salary bases, cost-of-living allowances would be suspended for retirees, pension contributions would rise, and the retirement age would be pushed from sixty to sixty-five. The union leaders were shocked by the proposals, especially the delayed retirement age.

A recent survey of nurses had shown a vast majority wanted the freedom to take retirement before they reached the eligible age of fifty-five. "I thought 'drive a stake in my heart, I can't take this to my members.' I was so mad I almost walked out of the room," Quinn said.

Quinn and Proulx-Daigle told the task force the terms were unacceptable, and both sides agreed to return to the drawing board. The early session made the unions suspicious of the government's motives. Was the task force simply a Trojan horse designed to strip away worker pension rights? The union leaders warned they would not cooperate with the government, their members' employer, unless it, too, was willing to put something on the table. Over the next weeks and months, the two sides inched toward an agreement. Alward's government agreed to increase contributions to the pension fund, but in exchange the unions had to swallow benefit reductions and other changes to ensure the long-term viability of their pensions. Rowland and the pension funds' long-standing actuary, Conrad Ferguson, played a key role in guiding the unions to the right mix of benefit cuts. Rowland's legal work with other unions and her partial success with Justice Grant earned the respect of Quinn and Proulx-Daigle. If she supported a benefit cut, they listened. They relied on Ferguson to test McCrossan's complex calculations about the long-term benefits of pension changes. "Conrad would come back to me and say, 'I'm very sorry to tell you this, but McCrossan is right, you are going to have to make this change to save the fund,'" Quinn said.

By March 2012, the task force and unions had reached an agreement on general terms of a new pension plan. They also had something else. Thanks to Rowland's shuttle diplomacy with other troubled New Brunswick pension funds, two more unions agreed to consider reforms. The New Brunswick Council of Hospital Unions joined the negotiating table after struggling for years with deficits. Union president Norma Robinson later told reporters her fund had tried to repair the plan, but "the resolve never seemed to come." Joining her was the New Brunswick Pipe Trade Union, headed by Gary Ritchie, representing the province's plumbers and pipefitters. Together, the pensions of the four unions represented more than twenty thousand workers and retirees.

Alward's government had decided it would not force its new pension model on the province's more than three hundred registered plans. It was too risky politically. All private and public sector pension plans were eligible to adopt the new model, but it was up to them to convince memberships. Given the precarious condition of pension plans, Alward was betting that the urgent need for a lifeline would give pension trustees the motivation to sell tough new benefit terms to members. Justice Grant's decision in 2011 put trustees on notice that they had a legal or fiduciary duty to act in the best long-term interests of all pension members.

The blueprint for New Brunswick's reforms came from the Netherlands. The Dutch had reformed their pensions in the early 2000s to prepare for the strain of baby boom retirements. The result was a shared-risk model that ranked as one of the world's most admired pension systems. McCrossan had studied the Dutch system. New Brunswick, he believed, had the potential to be Canada's Netherlands.

Like the Dutch model, the province's pension system would be called a shared-risk plan. Unlike traditional workplace plans that require employers to top up deficits, employees and retirees would now share the burden of fixing troubled pensions. Employers and employees would increase contributions if needed, and benefits could be scaled back or redesigned to ensure pensions had sufficient surpluses to survive market shocks and demographic changes. Unlike Conrad Ferguson's alarming 2009 prognosis that the plan for the two New

Brunswick unions would need to slash benefits by more than 60 per cent to save pension plans, most new reforms would be introduced incrementally. Those pensions that agreed to reforms would also have to adhere to more conservative risk management tactics – practices that would use more modern and conservative mortality and investment forecasts. Overly optimistic forecasts would no longer mask funding issues. Overseeing all these changes would be independent administrators.

The reform's most profound changes affected retirees. Planned new provincial legislation, the country's most sweeping pension reform in decades, would allow shared-risk pension plans to expropriate certain rights of retirees. If a fund was hit with a deficit, retiree benefits could be temporarily altered. For the four unions negotiating with the task force, the change meant both retirees' cost-of-living allowances and other active member benefits would become conditional. If their pension fund had a deficit, the contingent benefits would be suspended until a surplus was restored. This was the benefit cut that Justice Grant had rejected when the two unions asked for his direction in 2011. Now New Brunswick was changing its laws so that all members who joined the new model would shoulder their share of the pension repair bill.

Another major change was the retirement age. It would be pushed to sixty-five from sixty. Addressing the nursing union's concerns, this shift would be introduced gradually over a forty-year period, which meant the bulk of the union's older workers would only delay their retirements by a few months. New employees would take a bigger hit, retiring years later than their predecessors. Workers would also be asked to increase contributions to the pension fund. Keeping Alward's promise, the province also agreed to increase contributions. The nurses, for example, would see their average pension contributions increased to 7.86 per cent from 5.25 per cent, a jump matched by the province.

Reforms also downsized the formula for calculating pension values. Like most Canadian plans, New Brunswick pensions are typically calculated from a base salary that reflects an average of a worker's highest salary years. Some New Brunswick plans were so generous that workers could supersize their base by adding overtime payments. Under the new model, pension values would be calculated from a lower base, derived from a worker's average career salary, contingently adjusted for inflation. Overtime pay would no longer be added to the formula.

These and other reforms laid the foundation for risk management practices that McCrossan, the risk-conscious former insurance actuary, had been advocating for years. The Dutch pension system was ranked as one of the soundest pension system in the world because it had enforced many of the standards and practices that New Brunswick was now adopting. One of Canada's weakest provinces was building the foundations for the country's most secure pension fortresses.

Four union leaders flanked Premier Alward when he strode onto the stage at Fredericton's new conference centre on the morning of May 31, 2012. Walking with him was Marilyn Quinn, Susie Proulx-Daigle, Norma Robinson, and Gary Ritchie, heads of unions who were announcing their participation in the new shared-risk pension model. Government and union officials had kept a tight lid on negotiations, so media and union members were learning the details of the pension reforms for the first time. Alward wanted union leaders to show a united front. Many media had arrived expecting to hear conflict. Unions and governments were always waging war over pension changes.

Alward began the press conference by talking about the acute condition of the province's pension plans, which he revealed for the first time were no longer sustainable. "It is not fair or realistic to expect New Brunswick taxpayers to backstop" troubled funds, he said. As a result of "unprecedented" collaboration with the unions, workers were sharing the burden, allowing the province to build a stronger system "before crisis struck." Like so many times before in the province's difficult history, he said, New Brunswickers had come together in the face of adversity because "we are driven by both a fiercely independent spirit and deeply rooted sense of community."

There would be no labour confrontation with the government this day. Benefits had been traded for long-term security, and each of the union leaders understood their members' pensions were protected for the long-term. "The retirement system was in jeopardy," Quinn told reporters. "We're confident today that this new model will secure retirement security."

"A historic moment," chimed in Robinson, head of the hospital workers union.

The united Conservative Party–labour front became even more surreal when the press conference ended and Robinson effusively urged Alward and her union counterparts to lay their hands on hers. After nearly seven months of difficult negotiations with the province, Quinn and Proulx-Daigle were caught off guard by Robinson's gesture. Their surprise turned to disbelief when she pushed everyone's hands into the air and let out a war whoop, like a coach exhorting a sports team before a game. "I couldn't believe it," said Quinn, who was eager to get on an arranged telephone conference call to her members to explain details of the new pension plan. "I thought 'shoot me now' if my members see me doing this with the premier, I'm done.'"

Quinn and the others would have to wait a little longer to speak to members. Alward asked union leaders and Sue Rowlands, there on behalf of the task force, to walk with him across the street to the ornate Victorian-era legislature building, where he was scheduled to introduce a bill with the new pension reform laws. Expecting to watch the session from the gallery, the five were instead escorted to the carpeted floor of the Assembly Chamber, where they were given seats on a wooden bench facing Alward. After the premier gave a speech explaining the significance of the new shared-risk pension plan, which would also be applied that day to MLA pensions, Alward asked his guests to stand as he thanked them for their co-operation. As they rose, the two-storey chamber was soon filled with thunderous applause. Every attending MLA from the two elected Liberal and Conservative parties stood to give the unions and the labour lawyer a standing ovation. Stunned by the reaction, Rowlands, the hard-nosed labour lawyer, began to cry. "Other than the day I was married it was the happiest day of my life. No one was playing silly buggers with politics. New Brunswick was fixing its pensions."

Four weeks before Alward introduced the reforms, another pension chapter was closed. It was late afternoon on May 1, 2012, and John Ferguson was racing into the new Saint John courthouse. He had just heard the news. After fifty-five days of trial and six hours of waiting for the jury to finish deliberations, the seven men and women were returning, arriving so quickly that Ferguson's wife, Trish, was still at a friend's house with their three young children. He waited for the verdict in the courtroom with his sixty-eight-year-old mother, who was trembling. Ferguson put his hand on his mother's to calm her, but she did not stop.

The legal ordeal had been a huge strain on his family. He had continued to pester the city about pension problems for a year after the 2007 libel notice and then defiantly raised the stakes in 2008 by running for mayor. At the time, few local citizens paid attention to the city's pension problems. Ferguson lost to Saint John's incumbent Mayor Court, who was re-elected. Defeated and tired of the uphill pension battle, Ferguson moved his family to St. Stephen, a small community west of the city, where he began a new job as the town's manager.

The case followed him to St. Stephen. After work, he spent nights reading boxes of court materials or huddling with lawyers. The city's insurance policy covered legal expenses, but that did not stop the pension board from playing rough with its outspoken critic. On December 17, 2008, as he joined his wife and his mother to prepare a birthday celebration for his one-year-old son, a car appeared in the driveway. Expecting guests, Ferguson went outside and was met by a stranger who handed him a letter. It was another legal document. The city's pension board had placed a lien on his house because a $3,500 payment was overdue. "My mother sat down in her chair and started to cry. She thought I was ruining my life," he said.

The jury had been asked to reach a decision on four libel claims. The judge instructed them that they could only find Ferguson guilty of libel if they were convinced that he had acted with malice when defaming pension board members. The jury dismissed the first and second allegations, and when they dismissed the third, the most potentially damaging claim that related to his inflammatory 2005 remarks about pension fund "negligence," Ferguson bolted out of his seat and headed for the door. Tears streaming down his face, he began punching his wife's phone number into his cell phone. He didn't hear the jury dismiss the final claim.

When he heard his wife's voice, Ferguson blurted, "It's over. We won."

Thirteen days later, Saint John voters went to the polls to elect a mayor. Ivan Court, who had not lost an election in fourteen years, conceded defeat one hour after the polls closed. Mel Norton, a thirty-eight-year-old lawyer who promised to restore the financial health of the city and its pension plan, was elected by a landslide of more than 70 per cent of votes. Seven months after he was elected, Norton reached a deal with unions representing police officers, firefighters, and other employees to convert their critically injured pension plan into New Brunswick's new shared-risk pension plan model. Saint John was on the hook to pay about $12 million a year for the next decade to eliminate its remaining deficit. If the city had started increasing pension contributions to fix the deficit in 2005 when Ferguson sounded the alarm, it's likely the shortfall would have been significantly reduced within those four years.

Ferguson says he has no plans to move back to Saint John. He likes his new job and he has lots of ideas for St. Stephen. One of them is the province's shared-risk pension plan. The town is part of a multi-employer pension plan that is currently shouldering a $39 million deficit.

"We are looking to fix that," he said.

CHAPTER 3

RHODE ISLAND

Truth in Numbers

When Roger Williams fled religious and political persecution in Massachusetts in 1636, the clergyman chose as his sanctuary the shallow end of a deep-water Atlantic cove that would become Providence, the capital of Rhode Island. Williams, a vocal critic of rigid British church and state rules, banded with dissidents to found a community that allowed residents to choose their faith and vote on local rules. Williams was such a convincing defender of social freedoms that when King Charles II granted Rhode Island its 1663 charter, he agreed to give the region greater authority over its government than any other colony. Born out of dissent, Rhode Island would be shaped by a fierce spirit of independence.

A year before a Boston mob threw tea overboard in 1773, Providence residents attacked and burned a British schooner enforcing unpopular trade rules. Rhode Island was the first colony to reject British rule in 1776 and the last of the original thirteen colonies to sign the U.S. Constitution, holding out until the Bill of Rights entrenched individual liberties. The state, the smallest in the union, was one of the first to abolish slavery in 1784, ending decades of heavy trading in African slaves through its busy port.

With its autonomous spirit, Rhode Island was a breeding ground for entrepreneurs. A state built on shipping and farming saw opportunity in the Industrial Revolution reshaping Britain. In the early nineteenth century, local businesses recruited British immigrants with factory experience to build some of America's first factories. Former Derbyshire textile apprentice Samuel Slater so effectively memorized his British employer's cotton mill operations that when Rhode Island investors lured him away in the 1790s, he was able to recreate a cotton mill in Pawtucket, the first in the country. Slater's first mill and its vibrating spindles did such a brisk business in cotton thread and woven textiles that copycat mills proliferated. At their peak in the late 1800s, more than one thousand mills were operating in the state. To the British, the expat was "Slater the Traitor"; to U.S. president Andrew Jackson, he was "the father of the American Industrial Revolution."

Rhode Island's economic boom attracted manufacturers, consolidating a thriving base of textile, rubber, metal, jewellery, and chocolate producers. The local economy expanded so rapidly that immigrants were recruited from Europe, Quebec, and, eventually, Latin America. The rapid inflow of immigrants changed the nature of civic politics. Towns once sustained by farms were confronted with foreign-born citizens, tax hikes, and expensive civic projects to support new communities.

The changes sparked vigorous debates. Predictably, given the state's volatile nature, some dissenters broke away to start new communities. The town of Smithfield was divided into three communities in 1871 after farmers and pro-industrialists could not resolve differences. Smithfield largely stuck to its agricultural roots while the new towns of Lincoln and North Smithfield welcomed manufacturers. Dissent led to another breakup in 1895 when farmers in the north end of Lincoln objected to the expense of new streets, sewers, and lights for a small neighbourhood to the south that housed a growing population of foreign factory workers.[1] The neighborhood broke off and formed a new town, Central Falls, billing itself as the City of Dreams, an ambitious claim for a municipality that occupied little more than one square mile.

Rhode Island's municipal balkanization reached absurd levels in a thinly populated rural area of the state. Anchored by the town of Coventry, the region is served by a municipal government and three separate fire districts, each with its own staff and responsibility to collect taxes. By the mid-1900s, virtually all of the municipalities and tiny fire districts had something else: employee pension plans. Some of the funds are so small that its members couldn't fill a bus. The quirky system is so difficult to oversee that no one appears to have calculated the number of funds or total assets under administration. When the *Providence-Journal* recently tried counting the number of local government pension funds in the state, the newspaper gave up at 155. The system is so perplexing that banks sometimes confuse fire district accounts and accountants misdirect pension financial statements to the wrong district. With so much confusion and little external oversight, local pension funds are fertile ground for political shenanigans.

Rhode Island has more local governments per capita than almost any other state. There are thirty-nine municipalities serving a population of 1.1 million in a state so tiny that most towns are a half-hour drive from the capital. The average municipal population in Rhode Island is twenty-eight thousand, a small tax base for governments that are on the hook to pay salaries and pension benefits while maintaining schools, libraries, roads, and other infrastructure. In good times, fragmented local government was affordable. Expanding manufacturers hired more workers who acquired homes, driving up property values and local property tax revenues. When the state's industrial base began to erode in the 1970s, the decentralized system was inefficient and ill-equipped to withstand financial shocks. The only recourse for most communities was to raise property taxes, a desperate fiscal move in a state enduring sharp property value declines. By 2011, Rhode Island's property taxes, as a share of personal income, ranked as the fourth highest in the United States.[2] The state earned another dubious distinction in 2011: it was experiencing some of the nation's sharpest increases in pension liabilities.

Rhode Island is a generous employer. The largesse is a product of historically close ties between the state's unions and the Democratic Party, which has dominated local politics since the Depression. Unions are heavily represented on state and municipal retirement boards, and elected officials have viewed pension perks as politically expedient rewards for friends and supporters blessed with jobs. Annual payroll costs were low, and fat pension promises would be paid down the road by other administrations.

There are so many pension plans in the small state that at times it seems they compete to outdo one another in benefit improvements. Retirement ages were lowered so frequently that by the 1990s it was possible for many government workers to retire in their forties. In some towns, workers retired one day and picked up another government job the next, while still collecting a pension. Cost-of-living increases were so generous for retirees in some municipalities that pension cheques eventually exceeded salaries.

Rhode Island's pension economics soured in the 1970s when the state began losing core textile industries and other manufacturing jobs to lower-cost states and countries. The industrial era was ending and Rhode Island's economy went into a still painful, decades-long slump. The tough times did not stop politicians from continuing to hand out pension goodies. Times were bad, but few politicians worried about future pension bills. In 1991, Providence's long-standing mayor, Vincent "Buddy" Cianci, the Prince of Providence, was so indifferent to pension costs that he approved new cost-of-living allowance (COLA) benefits that hiked retirees' pensions by as much as 6 per cent annually.

The stunning raise was a windfall for some pensioners. By 2011, former Providence fire chief Gilbert McLaughlin was pocketing an annual pension of U.S.

$197,000, three times his annual salary of $63,000 when he retired in 1991. If McLaughlin lives to one hundred, his pension will be $700,000. When Providence became overwhelmed with declining revenues and soaring pension costs, Cianci's administration solved the financial crunch by suspending required contributions into employees' pension fund. "Everyone was doing it," Cianci told Public Broadcasting System (PBS) in 2011.[3]

The former mayor is right to say that a number of Rhode Island governments, including the state, often solved budgetary headaches by suspending pension contributions. The practice meant that the state with one of the nation's most expensive retirement systems had one of its worst funding records. The scale of funding neglect was bigger in Providence than anywhere else. By 2011, Providence's pension fund was only 34 per cent funded, leaving it with a staggering shortfall of $829 million. Cianci, who was sentenced to five years in jail in 2002 for corrupt government practices after he and a handful of city officials were nabbed in a sting called "Plunder Dome," is unrepentant about short-changing his city's pension plan. Currently working as a radio host in Providence, he told PBS: "There was only so much to spread around."[4]

It took more than thirty years of neglect for Rhode Island's pension system to implode. As early as 1974, an actuary warned the state that repeated annual funding deficits were threatening the survival of Rhode Island's largest pensions funds, covering state employees and teachers. In a rare moment of actuarial pique, the adviser chastised the state's politicians for pension complacency:

> Perhaps, mingled with these attitudes is the feeling that though future generations of employees may be affected, the problem is of no concern to present employees, a sort of "let the future take care of itself" psychology. Whatever may be the reason behind this lack of official and employee concern, the fact is that it is unrealistic. A change of attitude and remedial and corrective measures are imperative if the retirement system is to survive.[5]

Rhode Island did move in 1986 to adopt more rigorous actuarial standards to fund the pension plan, but its record of sticking to the rules was spotty. When the state was hammered with a credit union crisis in the early 1990s, it suspended required contributions to the plan for three years, a hole it later filled. The government turned a deaf ear to its actuary again in 1997 when he opposed the state's exuberant forecast that the fund would earn an investment return of 8.25 per cent. After fees, the actual return was 2.28 per cent, meaning the fund was earning less than a third of what was needed to pay pension obligations.

While state and local governments skimped on pension contributions, politicians spent lavishly on benefits. By the 1990s, state employees could retire on a full pension after twenty-eight years of service, regardless of age. The generous retirement policy, matched by some municipalities, sped an exodus of baby boom workers who had not contributed enough to their pension plans to pay the soaring retirement bill. When pension investment returns plunged after the dot-com bubble burst in 2001, Rhode Island could no longer feed the pension monster. The funding shortfall for the state pension system had grown so large that Rhode Island was left with two options: cut pension benefits or raise government contributions. Between 2004 and 2010, taxpayer contributions to the sickly pension fund doubled, to $302 million. Total taxpayer contributions to employee pensions soared from 5.6 per cent of salaries in 2002 to more than 20 per cent in 2010, while employee contributions were limited by statute to 9.5 per cent.

When the 2008 financial crisis and subsequent recession sent markets and global economies into a tailspin, Rhode Island had nothing left to give. By 2009, the state pension fund only had two-thirds of the assets required to meet pension promises, a funding gap repeated in many Rhode Island municipalities. It was time for the state to cut back. If it didn't slay the pension dragon, services would have to be cut.

In 2009 and 2010, local newspapers were filled with wrenching stories of government service cutbacks. Whiplashed by shrinking revenues and expanding pension debts, Rhode Island started slashing. Its biggest move was to eliminate revenue sharing and dramatically shrink local aid to municipalities, a key revenue source for many financially crippled towns and cities. Raising property taxes was no longer an option in a state where housing prices had plunged 27 per cent after the financial crisis. Bus routes were cut, library hours reduced or eliminated altogether, and government jobs were sharply trimmed. Still, the state's political leaders were not going anywhere near the third rail. It was more expedient politically to cut services and jobs in a state coping with an 11 per cent unemployment rate than to cut pension benefits.

One businesswoman was paying close attention to all the financial horror stories. Born and raised in Providence,

Gina Raimondo is the granddaughter of Italian immigrants who moved to Rhode Island to pursue the American Dream. One of her grandfathers was a cook who improved his English reading at a Providence public library. Her father, a Second World War veteran, went to college on a GI bill and landed a job as a metallurgist with a nearby Bulova watch factory. When Gina, the youngest of three children, was in sixth grade, her father lost his job when the watch factory shut down. Blindsided, her father was forced to retire with a sharply reduced pension, a loss that forced him to juggle a series of part-time jobs. The experience made a big impression on young Gina about the injustice of not warning workers about pension threats. Employees, she told *The New York Times* in 2011, needed time to make other plans. "You can't let people think that something's going to be here if it's not," she said.[6]

While her family adjusted to new circumstances, Gina Raimondo plowed her energies into school. Entering high school she made the daily seven-mile commute by bus. Nights and weekends she studied at the local library. Her hard work paid off. She went to Harvard, where she excelled in economics, won a Rhodes Scholarship to study at Oxford, and earned a law degree from Yale. A slip of a woman who barely touches five feet, she chose rugby as her college sport.

As she read the stories about service cutbacks in Rhode Island, Raimondo grew incensed. Buses and libraries had helped her family succeed for generations.

"I wouldn't be where I am without good government services," she said in an interview from her Providence office. "It's the American Dream. People can grow up working class and wind up at Harvard and Yale and Oxford. If we don't make this government work that kind of story just won't happen anymore."

A lifelong Democrat who entertained political ambitions, Raimondo believed she had the financial skills to fix the crisis. "I literally put the paper down and said, 'I have to fix this, I have to run,'" she would later tell *Bloomberg*.[7] Although she was active in local business and community groups, Raimondo had many reasons *not* to get involved. She had a busy job as one of the founders of Rhode Island's first venture capital firm, Point Judith Capital; she was also a volunteer director at a local homeless centre and had an active home life with two young children.

There were other obstacles, Raimondo's business friends and Democratic leaders warned. Rhode Island was on the verge of being bankrupted by its pension debts, and the only way to fix it would be to overhaul state laws. That meant taking on the unions, a suicide mission for Democratic politicians, who owed much of their support to labour groups. "Everyone said 'don't own the pension issue,' 'lead from behind,' 'stay away from this,' 'don't touch it,'" she said.

The tenacious former rugby player ignored the warnings. In 2010, Raimondo, then thirty-nine, campaigned for Rhode Island treasurer. Her core platform was fiscal and pension reform. The stand lost her the support of the powerful teachers union, but her message resonated with taxpayers. In November 2010, the political novice won by a landslide, garnering more votes than any other candidate for state office.

One of the first calls Raimondo received after she was sworn in as Rhode Island's treasurer in January 2011 was from the Securities Exchange Commission. The Washington-based regulator was investigating whether Rhode Island and other states and cities had accurately disclosed the full extent of their financial problems to government bond investors. The main focus of the probe was underfunded pension plans.

For the next month, the state's new treasurer closeted herself with a consultant accustomed to being ignored by politicians. Joe Newton is an actuary who advises a variety of state governments about their pension systems.

For most politicians, actuaries are about as much fun as dentists, drilling painfully into sickly pension funds and prescribing expensive repair work. Raimondo, however, is not most politicians. She estimates she spent more than one hundred hours with Newton in her office in the sprawling white marble state capital overlooking Providence. In the shadow of a multi-storey dome topped by an eleven-foot bronze statue dedicated to "The Independent Man," Rhode Island's state treasurer followed her own path. After days of struggling to understand the financial condition of the retirement system for state employees and teachers, she came to realize that the system no longer made sense. Years of mismanagement and underfunding had allowed money to be drained that was needed to pay promised pensions. The crisis was much worse than Raimondo had expected.

"This is really bad, what am I going to do?" she remembers thinking at the time. "The actuary was telling us that under a reasonable set of assumptions, this pension fund would pretty much be out of money in twenty to twenty-five years." To the trained economist, the math was horrifying: the state's retirement funds had only 56 per cent of the assets needed to pay more than $14 billion of pension liabilities. The money that was left was flying out the window because the state's pension members had not contributed enough to pay for lucrative pension benefits for the growing ranks of retirees, who almost outnumbered workers. Pension bills were costing Rhode Island 10 per cent of its annual payroll, a number Newton warned would double in a year. It was an unaffordable burden for a state that was facing a $300 million budget deficit in fiscal 2012. If pensions were going to be saved, the math had to change. To accomplish that, state lawmakers had to overhaul pension laws to reduce pension benefits. She would need voter support and she would need the backing of enough members from the Senate and House of Representatives to pass new legislation. This meant shifting Rhode Island's political mindset.

"This is all about the extremely hard challenge of getting people to think long-term," Raimondo said. "Historically, at least in this country, when people reform public pension systems, they approach it with a budgetary lens. They say, 'What changes do we have to make to the pension to balance the budget?' As a result what you see in most places is small tweaks to pensions."

Raimondo did not run for office to *tweak* the pension system. The state could not save its pensions unless they were dramatically restructured. To win support for her ambitious plan, she had to enlist Governor Lincoln Chafee, a one-time Republican who was voted into office after he ran as an independent. Chafee, fifty-eight at the time, agreed the pension crisis was strangling the state, but he had opposed cutting the benefits on the campaign trail. His solution was to delay the crisis by stretching out or amortizing payments on the $7 billion funding shortfall over thirty years.

To Raimondo, the governor's stand exemplified the type of political stalling tactic that had allowed the pension contagion to spread. His proposed delay would only further deplete assets needed to pay pension bills. She and her staff prepared presentations for the governor to convince him that the state had to downsize pensions. Rhode Island, she explained to Chafee, was living in a pension house it could not afford. Refinancing the mortgage would only cost more over the long-term and potentially leave employees and retirees with very little retirement savings.

If Chafee didn't back away from his plan, Raimondo warned she was prepared to go to war. "I said, 'Governor, I understand you're going to advocate for amortization and I just want you to know if you do that, I'll be vocally opposed,'" Raimondo recalled in an interview. To his credit, she says, Chafee listened.

The next step was to convince Rhode Island's voters. This meant telling working and retired state employees their pensions had to shrink – bad news that no politician wants to share with his or her constituency. For

Raimondo, the economist and financier, winning the debate meant ignoring the past. Yes, there had been mistakes and political mismanagement. Yes, most employees had upheld their bargain by regularly contributing to their pensions. If she was going to win support from her state, the treasurer decided, she had to strip away the emotions by focusing on the math. Explain the numbers and reasonable people could not disagree that the state was being strangled by its pension debts. Mathematically, she would tell local reporters, it was "impossible" to fix the traditional pension regime. Redesigning Rhode Island's retirement system, she said, "was an everybody issue." Everyone – taxpayers, workers, and retirees – were all in the same boat: they would suffer income cuts or tax increases if the system was not redesigned.

In May 2011, four months after she took office, Raimondo issued a startlingly frank pension manifesto. Titled *Truth in Numbers*, the sixteen-page report was a bleak chronicle of how pension mismanagement had bequeathed taxpayers a pension mortgage that could no longer be paid, while leaving retirees with a shaky retirement home that was on the verge of collapsing. The report did not flinch from the sacrifices that Raimondo believed were necessary to salvage what was left of the state's pension savings. Like New Brunswick, she wanted Rhode Island to borrow from the Dutch pension model and suspend cost-of-living allowances paid to twenty-one thousand retired state employees until the underfunded plan was largely replenished. Future pension benefits should be calculated from a salary base that was drawn from workers' average career income rather than the more costly base of their final income years. State employees would no longer be able to retire in their forties and fifties; the retirement age needed to be shifted to sixty-seven. The report explained the advantages of creating a new hybrid pension model that would roll workers' accrued defined pension benefits together with a new defined contribution plan. The state would honour the defined benefits that workers had already accumulated during their career, but going forward it would only commit to paying fixed contributions to a hybrid pension that combined old defined benefit savings with the new defined contribution plan The days of fully guaranteed pension benefits in Rhode Island were coming to an end.

Raimondo's pension solution ranks as the most radical in recent U.S. history. Although virtually every state was coping with pension shortfalls, a funding gap that easily exceeds $1 trillion, politicians have traditionally shied away from targeting retiree benefits.[8] In 2011, Raimondo did not shrink from necessary tough talk. Retirees who had been promised a fixed pension and cost-of-living allowances had to accept less if Rhode Island was going to salvage its retirement system. Pensioners were living much longer than plan designers had projected, and investment returns had been so disappointing that funds did not have enough assets to pay the swelling retirement bill. If benefits were not cut, pension funds would run out of money and retirement benefits for younger workers would evaporate. "Sugar coating only hurts people," Raimondo said. "This problem won't go away until you fix it. The longer you wait, the harder it will be to fix." Few politicians in other state and local governments had the stomach for her tough pension medicine, choosing instead to turn a blind eye when fault lines materialized.

For example, Prichard, a small town of twenty-three thousand on the Gulf Coast of Alabama, waited until its pension plan ran out of money before taking action in 2009, five years after actuaries predicted the crisis.[9] The town's solution was to stop sending pension cheques to one hundred and fifty retirees, a violation of state law that ultimately pushed the town into bankruptcy proceedings. Retirees went without any pension income for twenty months until they reluctantly struck an agreement in 2011 that slashed monthly payments by two-thirds, leaving them with meagre pensions paying an average of about $300 a month.

Towering pension debts helped push Vallejo, California, into bankruptcy in 2008. Although the city was being smothered by pension costs, its plan to cut benefits was derailed. The obstacle was the California Public Employees' Retirement System (CalPERS), the world's sixth-largest pension fund, overseeing more than $250 billion of pension savings for state employees. After the fund threatened a multi-year legal battle to stop the deeply troubled city from touching members' pensions, Vallejo backed away and instead cut services. Police officers were laid off, fire stations closed, and City Hall staff gutted.

CalPERS has successfully stared down a handful of other local municipalities that sought to trim pension benefits, but it is losing a much bigger battle. Its pension liabilities are growing so much faster than its assets that its actuary reported in 2013 that CalPERS's various funds were between 60 per cent and 80 per cent short of assets needed to pay pension obligations. CalPERS's board voted to fix the shortfall in April by raising state contributions to employee pensions by 50 per cent over the next six years. The demand is wildly out of sync with the frail fiscal condition of a state that has seen four municipalities topple into bankruptcy and many more struggle to pay school and other essential services.

Rhode Island's unions borrowed a page from CalPERS's playbook when it launched a campaign in the summer of 2011 to oppose the treasurer's reforms. The teachers union that refused to back Raimondo during the state election rallied workers against her proposal. A more vocal opponent was Council 94, the local union that represents state, county, and municipal workers in Rhode Island.

Michael Downey gets red in the face when he talks about pension reform. He is a big bear of a man with an unruly tangle of grey hair that he rakes with his hands when he gets aggravated. Like his father, Downey is a plumber who worked his way to the top of a union to bargain for better benefits. His father was president of Rhode Island's plumbers union, and today Downey is president of Council 94, which represents about ten thousand active and retired state employees. He has little tolerance for talk about pension cuts because he says many of his members can barely pay their bills with pensions that pay on average $22,000 a year. One month after Raimondo issued her *Truth in Numbers* report, Downey was leading a "fight back" campaign that demonized the state government for attacking collective bargaining rights.

Sitting in his modest office near Providence, Downey is quick to agree that Rhode Island's pension finances are "a mess." The crisis, he explains, is the fault of the state's political, judicial, and police leaders, who created "a little fantasy club" that allowed the most richly paid employees to "abuse" the pension system. Rhode Island state police and judges earn some of the state's highest pensions and, until recently, were not required to make personal contributions to their plans. Downey can't see beyond this injustice. When asked about the perilous underfunding of state pension funds, he dismissively waves his hand and says, "This is not my members' fault, why should they pay?" What about Rhode Island's pension lapses, including unrealistically low life expectancy projections that, until recently, fell well below modern projections of about eighty-one years? Downey growls, "I take umbrage with that. I'm constantly going to wakes, I don't know anyone that lives that long."

Faced with union opposition, Raimondo took her reform pitch on the road, visiting more than one hundred community centres, town halls, immigrant clubs, and schools during the summer and fall of 2011 to tell crowds of disgruntled workers and retirees why they had to accept smaller pension benefits. At most meetings, retirees, workers, and labour leaders angrily denounced the state for breaking pension contracts employees had faithfully honoured with regular pension contributions. When workers shouted her reform was "immoral," she retorted it was immoral to cut vital school and transportation services. She had so thoroughly researched local property tax rates in Rhode Island municipalities that she was able to tell any retiree who opposed pension cuts how much their taxes would increase in the next year if the benefits were not scaled back. Few could dispute her math, and even union opponents such as Robert Walsh, executive director of the National Education Association, the state teachers union, marvelled to reporters that she was "fearless."

Raimondo had three things going for her in the uphill pension battle. Under Rhode Island law, state pension benefits are approved by the legislature. They are not part of a collective bargaining process, which means the government could argue, if legally challenged, that cutting pension benefits did not violate labour contracts. Another advantage was a tactical legal move by the state to restrict potentially unruly local governments from damaging Rhode Island's credit rating. In July 2011, Rhode Island's legislature passed a unique new law retroactively guaranteeing that all investors in state or municipal bonds would be fully repaid first in the event of a government bankruptcy. While some municipalities complained the state was putting Wall Street ahead of Main Street, the move ensured that Rhode Island and other local governments could continue raising badly needed funds by selling bonds. If one municipality declared bankruptcy, it would not be able to dig out of the hole by reneging on bond payments.

A few weeks after the law was passed, one of Rhode Island's poorest cities sought bankruptcy shelter from a pension volcano that had been spewing ominously for years. The harsh solution for the critically wounded city would send a chilling message about the dangers of ignoring unpaid pension bills.

Central Falls has been a municipal castoff since 1895 when the rural town of Lincoln hived off a small southern pocket that housed immigrant factory workers. A postage stamp of a city, Central Falls was for decades a densely populated blue-collar town of 1.3 square miles, overflowing with European immigrants who worked in nearby textile factories. When industries moved away in the 1970s, unemployment soared, housing prices sank, and immigrants from Colombia, Puerto Rico, and Mexico poured into the declining city. In 1986, crime became such a dominant local industry that *Rolling Stone* magazine crowned Central Falls the "Cocaine Capital of New England."

On August 2, 2012, the City of Dreams earned another title: Pension Wreck of the Year. On that day, Central Falls stepped into the nightmare of bankruptcy protection because it had no money left to pay more than

$40 million in pension obligations to retired and active city workers. The retirement bill was staggering for a city with a paltry annual budget of $16 million and a tiny pool of only 314 active and retired workers.

The Central Falls employee pension plan suffered from many of the same afflictions that damaged other state and municipal funds. Its political leaders were overly generous with retirement terms and lax about saving enough to pay the bills. Central Falls took these practices to a whole new level of recklessness. Since the early 1990s, city employees had been allowed to retire after working as little as twenty years on the job. Terms for local police were particularly generous. According to court-appointed staff who managed the city after its bankruptcy filing, about 60 per cent of the city's police officers who retired since the early 1990s had been granted a disability pension, which allowed them to retire early and shield about two-thirds of their pension income from taxes. The average retirement age of disabled police workers was forty-six, and many went on to find full- or part-time employment elsewhere. The luckiest police pensioner was arguably Joseph Moran, Central Fall's chief of police. On March 23, 2010, Moran retired with a pension of $50,600 at the age of forty-seven. The next day, according to court documents, the city's mayor hired Moran as a colonel under a five-year contract that paid $80,000 annually and included such perks as the tuition costs on his masters of business degree. Moran was allowed to continue earning his pension during the contract.

Central Falls was a poor saver for its rich retirement promises. It frequently failed to make contributions to employee pension funds, and when the money got tight, it did little to boost revenues. According to an investigation by John Hill of the *Providence Journal*, Central Falls repeatedly ignored warnings from its actuary that the city was not saving enough money in its pension funds.[10] Raising property taxes, which accounted for 75 per cent of the city's income, would have been the logical solution, but a succession of mayors opted to avoid politically unpopular tax hikes. Between 1991 and 2009, Central Falls raised its property taxes by 3.2 per cent. During the same time, Rhode Island's municipalities hiked taxes by more than 100 per cent, according to the *Providence Journal*.

The distressed city was able to mask its underfunded pension plan for years because it received millions of dollars of aid annually from the state. When the 2008 financial crisis pushed Rhode Island to the brink, the state was forced to eliminate municipal aid payments that accounted for about one-third of Central Falls' annual income. Without the safety net, Central Falls could no longer pay pensions owed to 141 retirees and placed itself in receivership in May 2010. A town with more than $40 million in pension obligations only had $4 million of assets in its employee pension funds.

For U.S. municipalities, receivership is the final stop before bankruptcy. In Rhode Island, receivership gives the state authority to intervene in distressed governments by working with a court-appointed receiver. Typically, receivers assess local finances and propose a road map of budget cuts, tax increases, and other measures to fix the mess. When Mark Pfeiffer, a retired judge who was appointed receiver in July 2010, issued his report later that year, he concluded that Central Falls' financial problems were "too large and too deep" to repair with conventional solutions. The best hope for the broken city was to merge with nearby Pawtucket.

The state's new governor, Lincoln Chafee, handed the difficult task of saving Central Falls in early 2011 to Robert Flanders, a Providence-based litigator and former judge with the state's Supreme Court who was a stranger to receiverships and restructurings. "I couldn't even find my way to bankruptcy court," he later said in an interview. Flanders initially responded that it would be a "thankless" job to serve as the ailing city's receiver. Governor Chafee, however, convinced him the job was too important to reject. Central Falls was one of many

Rhode Island municipalities being crushed by pension debts; if they could fix the little city, they could press for similar changes in other towns. "He asked me if I would take on this project because he thought it would be the biggest issue his administration would face. . . . It seemed like an impossible Herculean labour to get this done."

What Flanders lacked in experience, he made up for in determination. His first step was to approach Pawtucket about a merger, but the neighbouring town was quick to reject the plan. The only remaining alternative was cost-cutting. Brusque and outspoken, Flanders took a sharp knife to the city's costs, quickly earning him the fury of sidelined city politicians and employees who seemed unwilling to take responsibility for Central Falls' perilous financial condition. While Central Falls' long-serving mayor Charles Moreau pled for a bailout from the state and other politicians talked of renegotiating more than $20 million in city bond debts, Flanders began shrinking the city.[11] He terminated the city's expensive new police colonel, former police chief Moran. The local library and community centre were shuttered, and about a third of the city's 174 jobs were eliminated by layoffs and attrition. The painful cuts, however, were not enough to stop the hemorrhaging. If the city was going to survive, it had to tackle its biggest cost, pensions.

Before Flanders could consider shrinking retirement benefits, he and his team needed to analyze the city's two pension funds. That job fell to Gayle Corrigan, a former McKinsey & Co. consultant who had just returned to her home in Rhode Island after years of work repairing struggling manufacturers in Russia. Hired as the city's chief of staff, Corrigan was tasked with compiling a financial analysis of the city's finances and pension plans. Typically, the job is a simple matter of punching electronic data into specialized computer programs. She soon discovered there was nothing simple about the city's bookkeeping. Its computerized payments system was so primitive that when an invoice was entered, a cheque was automatically issued. When she asked a manager for accounts receivable statements, the employee opened a desk drawer and handed her batches of invoices. To calculate city cash flow, she sifted through a maze of bank accounts. When she finished counting, she learned Central Falls had fifty-four bank accounts with just a few million dollars of cash. Central Falls, she concluded in an interview, was in worse condition "than any Russian company I had worked for. It was overwhelming."

Her next task was more challenging. She had to add up the city's pension obligations to retirees and active workers. Nobody had a complete record, and it took days of hunting through filing cabinets and bank records in the three-storey red brick City Hall to find stray records of pension members and their benefits. The final tally, reached in early July 2011, was stunning. In a few weeks, Central Falls would be out of money to pay its debts. Its options were limited. The state had not responded to Mayor Moreau's pleas for a bailout and its bond debts were untouchable after the state had passed, earlier that month, legislation protecting bondholders. "We had just run out of time, the retirees were going to get whacked because no one had paid attention to the problem," she says.

Backed by Rhode Island's government, Flanders delivered a brutal message to employees and retirees who were invited to a meeting on July 19. Standing in the suffocating afternoon heat of the Central Falls High School auditorium, Flanders, sweating profusely in a short-sleeved white shirt and suspenders, explained the city's dire financial condition to about one hundred gathered retirees and workers. With virtually no money left to pay the pension bill, Flanders, flanked by two state police officers, told the hushed crowd he had to make "a big ask." Workers and retirees who were receiving or due to receive pensions of more than $10,000 a year would have to give up as much as 50 per cent of their pensions. "There is simply no money in the city to continue on the current path," he said. If pension members didn't agree to the cuts within seven days, he warned that Central Falls would be forced into bankruptcy and pensioners could suffer much bigger losses.

He was greeted with a barrage of angry cries and a long line of retirees, most of them former police officers in their fifties and sixties, waiting to have their say at the microphone. "Where is the fairness?" said one retired police officer. Added another police retiree: "The city, through their callousness and everything else, just blew it."

Sitting near the back of the sauna-hot auditorium was Bruce Ogni, a forty-seven-year-old former police captain who had retired six years earlier on a disability pension after he blew out both his knees "chasing down criminals" on the streets of Central Falls. "When someone stands there and tells you they are going to take 50 per cent of your pension, you can't believe it," he said in an interview nearly two years after the steamy meeting. Ogni agrees that benefits, particularly cost-of-living allowances for retirees, were "out of control," but he is appalled that the city "put a shotgun to our heads" and gave them a scant week to digest the shocking news. He didn't like the message and liked the messenger even less. Speaking in a thick New England accent, Ogni said Flanders "has no hawt."

Flanders stood his ground against the angry crowd. He warned them they were better off approving his harsh medicine than gambling with steeper losses in bankruptcy proceedings. Choosing an unfortunately harsh analogy, he said, "I would advise you that a haircut still looks a lot better than a beheading." Ten days later, on July 29, all but two of Central Falls' 141 retirees voted in favour of a beheading. Three days later, Flanders, on behalf of Central Falls, filed for bankruptcy protection under Chapter 9 of the U.S. Bankruptcy Code, marking the first municipal filing in the state's history.

A cold rain was falling hard when a red Mini Cooper pulled into the Chariho Middle School parking lot in the early evening of November 16, 2011. The squat brick school serves students from three local towns in a heavily wooded rural region about forty minutes south of Providence. Chariho's vision statement promises a "warm and welcoming place" for all students and adults. On this gloomy night the policy would not be honoured. As soon as Gina Raimondo and her communications adviser, Joy Fox, stepped out of the small car, they knew they were headed for battle. Dozens of people sporting stickers from the state union for teachers, one of the most vocal critics of Raimondo's pension reforms, were filing into the school's auditorium.

Dressed in a grey-flecked dress and red jacket, Raimondo barely drew applause when she joined a handful of local Democratic representatives on stage. She began with a brief introduction she had repeated dozens of times in similar sessions that summer and fall to explain why the state was reducing pension benefits. "It's not about taking pensions away," she explained, it is about "security." If everybody didn't agree to take their share of cuts, the pension funds would run dry. Her audience wasn't listening to the math. This was their last chance to vent because the next day the state's General Assembly and Senate were due to vote on the pension reforms. Retirees lined up at the microphone to unleash a barrage of complaints. One raged against unfair six-figure pensions earned by judges. Another calculated he would lose nearly $100,000 of income in his final years because of the planned suspension of cost-of-living allowances. Some fumed that the state and Raimondo were acting immorally by yanking away retirement benefits they had collected for years. Raimondo patiently listened to each speaker and lingered after to speak individually to retirees who approached her with questions.

She winces to this day when she recalls the confrontations that night. "They all beat up on me, one after another," she said. "But you know what? I stayed. I stood there. I answered the questions." The only crack in Raimondo's steely resolve occurred in the car as she and Fox pulled away from the school. Sensing her boss's fragility, Fox, always mindful of Raimondo's disciplined eating habits, made a pitch for comfort food.

"Can we have French fries just this one night?"

"Yeah," Raimondo replied, "we can do French fries."

The two women digested their greasy snack at the state capital. Although most of her colleagues in the Democratic Party were confident that they had enough support to pass the reforms, Raimondo wasn't taking anything for granted. It was a good bet that some representatives would seek to mollify angry labour groups with last-minute amendments to a new pension system modelled on Raimondo's *Truth in Numbers* report. The major changes included gradually raising the retirement age to sixty-seven, suspending cost-of-living allowances until pension fund surpluses were mostly restored, and converting existing pensions to hybrid defined benefit/contribution plans. These reforms would be watered down if state politicians, seeking to mollify labour groups, passed amendments that rolled back some of the pension cuts. The state was on the eve of such an historic pension overhaul that reporters from national television and print outlets, including *Time Magazine*, *The New York Times*, and *The Wall Street Journal*, had flown in to witness the vote. All of them wanted to interview

Raimondo. She and Fox had to be prepared if the vote went the wrong way.

A lot had happened in the ten months since Raimondo was sworn into office in January. Her *Truth in Numbers* report and local town hall meetings had touched a chord with the state's weary taxpayers. Voters had run out of patience with high local taxes and deteriorating government services. This was no longer a Tea Party or Republican issue; the political narrative had changed in the state. Democrats were facing a backlash if they continued to avoid fixing a broken retirement system.

Labour opposition had also lost some momentum after Central Falls. As Flanders had predicted, bankruptcy was devastating for retirees. The Chapter 9 proceeding gave Flanders the legal right to shred labour contracts and rewrite pension terms. Four months after the bankruptcy filing, the city's 141 retirees voted in December to accept a new pension contract that would slash their retirement incomes by as much as 55 per cent a year. Rhode Island would help ease the pain of the losses for the first five years by paying most retirees a supplement of a few thousand dollars a year annually. Just as the Nackawic pension collapse in New Brunswick had shattered the illusion that pension plans were a guarantee, Central Falls sent a message to other state and municipal employees that they could be next if their pension houses were not repaired. More than a dozen Rhode Island municipalities, including the state capital Providence, were reassessing pension costs that were pushing them to the brink.

Just as Raimondo had predicted, Rhode Island's House of Representatives was busy with floor amendments when the new pension legislation was tabled shortly after 2:30 p.m. the next day. During the next several hours, more than thirty amendments were introduced, many of them attempts to shield various pension members from the changes. Watching the political theatre from a second-floor gallery were more than two hundred spectators, most of them union officials, including Council 94 president Michael Downey. As the procession of amendments were voted down, a chorus of jeers and catcalls from the gallery grew so loud that the House speaker warned them to be silent.

House Majority Leader Nicholas Mattiello stood to soothe the crowd: "Nobody woke up one morning and said, 'We're going to take something from folks.' Most of the folks up in the gallery are our friends." He was drowned out by booing. Near the end of the session he stood again. "We have a $7.3 billion pension liability. . . . Whether you are sitting in this room or voting, you are one of the employees who is going to be impacted. It has to be done. We had no choice." At 7:40 p.m., more than five hours after the legislation was introduced, the vote was called. It was a landslide: fifty-seven representatives voted in favour and fifteen opposed. A few minutes later, the Senate delivered a bigger sweep, with thirty-two in favour and two opposed.

Raimondo, who had been tensely watching the debate from her office television, was suddenly the most sought-after politician in the United States. Reporters lined up outside her suite of offices to interview the political novice who had accomplished the seemingly impossible in a discouraging era of American political gridlock. She had convinced politicians to risk their political careers to secure a financially sound, long-term future for the state and its retirees.

"Government worked tonight," she told reporters. "On one of the toughest, most financially complicated, politically charged issues we face, we did something right."

CHAPTER 4

THE NETHERLANDS

The Polder Model

During its early history the boggy lowlands that became the Netherlands was a battleground for Romans, Germanic tribes, Vikings, and Spaniards who wished to rule the strategic coastline. The land was never truly conquered, however, until the thirteenth century, when enterprising local farmers defeated an even more determined enemy: water. For much of its early history, the Netherlands was submerged beneath swamps and lakes. Early farmers recovered some land by manually draining and diverting the water to nearby rivers. The strategy worked until the peaty soil decomposed after prolonged contact with air and sun, pushing a quarter of the country below sea level. As farmlands sank, fear of flooding became a national obsession. The war against water was not led by generals but rather grassroots collectives of farmers. Their constant attention to water levels shaped a unique collective national character.

Polder is the Dutch word for reclaimed lands, and the ingenious process for averting floods is called the polder system. Initially, farmers erected dykes and pumping systems to keep out unwanted tidal waters. One farmer's solution, however, became another's crisis when dykes burst or rechannelled waters gushed onto nearby fields. The need for coordination and caution was permanently etched into the national psyche in 1421 when dykes near Dordrecht were breached during a violent storm, unleashing a devastating flood that submerged villages, killing thousands of residents. If water was going to be tamed, the Dutch understood, farmers, villagers, and political leaders had to work together.

As early as the thirteenth century, collectives known as water boards, or *waterschappen,* were formed to organize the supervision of dykes and water levels. In a time of kings and noblemen, these co-operatives were the first form of democratic government in the Netherlands. Board members were often elected, and their rules were the product of constant discussion and debate. Landowners and tenants pitched in to fortify dykes, dig canals, build windmills, and install pumping stations to drain water. The triumph of the collective is best captured in the national saying: "God created the earth, but the Dutch created the Netherlands."

The Dutch triumph over the seas produced another dividend: early experiments with co-operatives inspired a tradition of political consensus known as the polder model. Compromise and bargaining became a way of life. The Dutch Republic was created in 1581 after seven provinces overcame their differences to unify. The country has a tradition of robust, diverse political parties – so diverse that governments are inevitably formed through coalitions. Few major economic initiatives are introduced without lengthy consultations involving employers and trade unions. One hugely successful collective undertaking occurred in the late 1940s when a new coalition government led the nation from the devastation of Nazi occupation to a new social welfare state. At the heart of the new order was a visionary pension policy that laid the seeds for one of the world's most admired retirement systems.

The father of the Dutch pension system is Willem Drees, a moderate socialist who began his career as a bank teller in the early 1900s. Drees left banking to set up his own business as a freelance stenographer, landing him a contract with the House of Representatives. The experience coupled with his mastery of a new shorthand language, based on noting core messages, would serve him well in the political arena. He joined the Social Democratic Party (a forerunner to the Labour Party) and slowly rose through the ranks as a pragmatic strategist who nudged the party from anti-establishment diatribes to constructive efforts to create jobs during the Depression. His ability to work with business to boost employment through public works projects broadened the popularity of a party that was lost in the wilderness. In 1933, at the age of forty-seven, he was one of a few Social Democrats elected to the Lower House. Six years later, the former bank teller was named leader of the party.

Drees's political ascent was cut short in 1940 when German soldiers invaded the Netherlands and outlawed socialist and communist political parties. After a year of imprisonment he went underground to serve as the head of the Social Democrats. His efforts to channel foreign aid to the needy and to help prepare the country for liberation earned him a post as the minister of social affairs in the emergency cabinet formed after the war.

In a country scarred by the occupation, one of Drees's first initiatives was to provide temporary retirement refuge for elderly who were destitute after two decades of economic decline. According to one of his biographers, Drees learned the importance of pensions as a child when his father's early death left his mother with no means to support her family of three children.[1] The bank employing his father agreed to provide her with a small pension in exchange for a promise that Drees would work at the bank for three years after graduating from school. The pension pact helped keep his struggling family afloat and gave Drees an early appreciation of the pension safety net.

Drees introduced an emergency retirement act in 1947 that handed destitute Dutch citizens over the age of sixty-five a modest government pension. The plan became so synonymous with its political author that pensioners referred to their benefits as "drawing money from Drees." His popularity carried a coalition of parties led by his party to power in the 1948 elections. During his next ten years in office, Drees emerged as one of the most unique political leaders of his era.

Sixty years old when he was elected, the legendary penny-pincher declined a government chauffeur or car and walked or cycled to his office. Politically, he was a realistic idealist. He advocated social welfare reforms but restrained trade unions and workers from strikes or wage hikes to help struggling employers compete globally. Like early polder regimes, everyone was encouraged under Drees's leadership to pitch in to keep the frail economy afloat. The balanced approach shaped the most enduring reform of his administration: a series of pension laws that became the building blocks for a retirement system that was so resilient it would require little change for decades.

The centrepiece of Drees's pension reform was the National Old Age Pensions Act (AOW), which extended a permanent retirement safety net for long-term residents of the Netherlands. The so-called "social minimum" plan operated like an insurance policy. Workers between the ages of fifteen and sixty-five paid regular premiums to build up their entitlement to a full pension. Unemployed or low-income workers were eligible for the pensions and the government effectively paid their premiums. Every eligible senior citizen was guaranteed a pension that is equivalent to the country's net minimum wage. Today the plan pays a monthly pension of about 1,000 euros for a single person and about 1,400 euros per couple. Drees placed a priority on a simple state pension so that every resident could easily understand what their base income would be in retirement. The flat payment structure accomplished something else: it put almost everyone in the same pension boat. Whether wealthy or poor, virtually all Dutch residents have the same stake in a national pension plan. Whenever the system needs fixes, there is a shared interest in ensuring long-term sustainability.

The second pillar of Drees's pension model was workplace pensions. The Social Democrat who earned his political stripes balancing employee and corporate interests took a similar approach to modernizing occupational pensions. Employee pensions in the Netherlands can be traced back to the Middle Ages, when enlightened guilds demanded contributions from tradesmen to support sick and elderly members.[2] Like employers in other industrialized nations, Dutch businesses started offering pensions in the late 1800s to retain workers in expanding factories. Drawing on the Netherlands' history of collective action, some companies took retirement plans a step further by joining forces to pool pension savings. The strategy gave employers more bargaining power to negotiate lower rates from insurance companies, then the primary source of pension investments. The first industry-wide retirement plans began appearing at the end of the First World War when insurance, mining, and graphic arts companies joined ranks to form pension collectives. The government attempted similar economies of scale in 1922 when it founded ABP, the goliath plan for all civil servants and education workers that now oversees one of the world's largest retirement funds.

Drees accelerated the shift to pooled funds with a series of new laws requiring all businesses in specified sectors to join a collective pension plan after 60 per cent of employers in that industry agreed to the arrangement. Participation was then mandatory for all businesses and employees. The big advantage for joining industry pension collectives was that it eliminated compensation competition. In pooled plans, pension terms are negotiated through a unique collective bargaining process during which trade unions and employers set terms for industry-wide pension benefits. The approach effectively set common contribution rates and benefit levels in each industry.

Prime Minister Drees reinforced the pension system by introducing strict funding and governance rules. Unlike in North America, for example, where exuberant bosses often paid little attention to how they were going to fulfill future pension promises, the Netherlands has for decades required rigorous funding standards. Workplace pension plans had to be fully funded, meaning they were required to have enough assets set aside to pay pension obligations. Oversight of the funds was transferred outside companies to organizations known as foundations, or *stichting*. Foundation boards were made up of an equal number of employee and employer representatives responsible for governing pension funds. The system restricted the ability of employers to meddle with pension savings, shielding Dutch plans from many of the abuses and poor management practices that toppled or threatened North American plans in recent years. There have been no Nackawics or Central Falls in the Netherlands.

Drees's pension model laid the foundation for a sturdy pension system that few could have imagined in the recovering postwar nation. Today more than 90 per cent of Dutch employees are members of a workplace retirement plan. The wide coverage has enabled a small country of 17 million people to build one of the world's richest pension systems. Its pension plans currently oversee more than CAN$1.3 trillion of assets, adding up to about 140 per cent of the country's total output, or gross domestic product (GDP). The ratio is higher than that of any other country, according to the Organisation for Economic Co-operation and Development (OECD). Canada, a nation of 34 million people, has about $1 trillion of pension assets amounting to 64 per cent of its GDP. The vast wealth has made Dutch retirees the richest pensioners in Europe, with the average pension equalling about 75 per cent of the nation's average wage.[3]

The massive pension pot was built to fund the costs of very generous pension plans, the large majority of which are defined benefit schemes that promise to pay a fixed pension for life at a given age. It is also a tribute to the cautious strategies of the country's large private and public sector pension plans, which place as much emphasis on managing pension funding risks as they do generating investment returns. Market turmoil in the past decade has confronted the pension system with its greatest funding challenges since it was created in the 1950s. These pressures are reshaping Drees's generous pension vision, but the Netherlands' pension challenges pale compared with those in most other countries.

The durable pension system is not the only legacy of Drees's vision. The extensive reach of workplace pensions has protected the Netherlands from divisions that poison the pension debate in many other nations. There is no rancorous divide between those who have pensions and those who don't because more than 90 per cent of workers are enrolled in plans. The other advantage is that trade unions and employers have jointly managed pension funds since the 1950s. Controversies and heated disagreements are common, particularly in recent years, but after more than 40 years of working alongside each other, employees and employers are experienced consensus builders. The shared history is the glue that has held together a remarkably resilient regime. The sharp decline of secure defined benefit pension plans in the

United States and Canada is often linked to the decline of union membership. This hasn't been the case in the Netherlands, where only a quarter of workers are union members. For decades labour and management have shared the same interest in a sustainable retirement promise. Their solidarity would be tested when financial storms breached the pension dykes in the 2000s.

The affluent seaside town of Noordwijk is known for endless sandy beaches, rugged dunes, and luxury villas. In November 2002, the village also became momentarily famous as the place where the curtain came down on the golden age of Dutch pensions. Delivering the message was Dick Witteveen, the then fifty-three-year-old head of the Dutch pension regulator. An intense man with owlish glasses, Witteveen had earned a reputation as a flinty and brusque regulator. He had previously led an ambitious overhaul of the country's tax code. In 2001, he was appointed chairman of the pension regulator just as the system was being thrashed by unprecedented investment losses in the dot-com crash. The country's average funding ratio of pension assets to liabilities dropped from 150 per cent in 1999 to 110 per cent in 2002.[4] Hidden within these numbers were funding shortfalls at hundreds of Dutch pension plans totalling more than 20 billion euros.[5]

Witteveen saw more than a funding crisis. Stock market losses exposed deep fault lines that threatened retirement promises Dutch workers had long taken for granted. The combined impact of plunging investment returns, expensive pension promises, and the onset of baby room retirements would be devastating if pension plans did not adhere to more rigorous regulations. Witteveen had telegraphed his concerns two months earlier in September 2002 in an extraordinary eleven-page letter to the country's pension plan managers. The blunt missive scolded managers for failing to save enough to weather such market shocks as the dot-com crash. The crisis had left the system vulnerable to future upheavals that could unravel the Dutch pension system if immediate steps were not taken. "The world has changed," he wrote, and the current state of the country's retirement system "was not acceptable."

When the letter was leaked to the media, Witteveen became entangled in a frenzied national debate. The country with the richest pension regime began debating the costs, durability, and design of its pension system. For the first time since the dark days of the Second World War, employees and retirees began fretting about retirement incomes.

To avoid media glare, Witteveen asked dozens of pension managers, employers, and labour representatives to meet with him in a confidential session. The setting was a remote conference centre in Noordwijk, about forty minutes southwest of Amsterdam. Despite the public controversy, he did not shrink from advocating harsh measures he believed were necessary to repair the country's venerated retirement system. Dutch pensions, Witteveen told the startled crowd, were "heading for a cliff." Pension plans were making promises they couldn't keep. Part of the problem was the legacy of generous early retirement policies in the 1980s and a shortsighted funding policy in the 1990s that kept employee contributions to pensions at about 4 per cent of their payroll. The collapse of technology stocks had unmasked these weaknesses, and the country would have to pay more to sustain its treasured retirement regime.

Witteveen sternly informed the room that the government was increasing regulatory supervision and imposing more stringent funding and investment standards – steps that would raise costs and reduce pension benefits. The biggest change would be a new rule that required funds to build a cushion for future financial shocks by accumulating a surplus – assets would have to be at least 105 per cent of pension liabilities. Even though many funds were still digging out of deficit holes from the dot-com crash, Witteveen said the new surplus rule would take effect in 2004.

The protests started before Witteveen was finished. *The regulator had no right to do this! It was a game-changer! Employees and employers would have to pay bigger pension contributions! Funding problems were overexaggerated!* While the room erupted with angry remarks, at least one person had a different response.

"I thought to myself, 'Boy, this guy has a lot of guts,'" said Keith Ambachtsheer, a Rotterdam-born, Toronto-based pension adviser who has championed Canadian pension reforms to mostly deaf political ears. "He had this steely resolve that this had to be done."

Dirk Broeders, a senior strategy adviser with the Dutch central bank who was then Witteveen's research assistant, said his boss put his reputation on the line by pushing for harsher, more costly rules. "He was prepared to take the blame as a regulator for the flaws in the system. He exposed his reputation and left himself vulnerable."

The early days of pension reform were rocky. As social partners studied and debated the mix of funding hikes and benefit cuts that would be needed to fortify pension plans, workers grew infuriated at the prospect of eroding pension benefits. If regulators had their way, the retirement age would be eventually pushed beyond sixty-five years, pension contributions would rise, and, for those that understood the shift, traditional benefits such as inflation protection would be conditional. The rage came to a head on October 2, 2004, when more than two hundred thousand protestors marched several blocks from Amsterdam's historic Dam Square to a park flanked by museums housing the nation's fabled Van Goghs and Rembrandts. Led by union leaders carrying street-wide banners reading "Stop the Tide of Destruction" and "Stop the Demolition," protestors railed against pension and social welfare cuts. One demonstrator carried a giant handmade sign of a worker being carried out of his office in a coffin because he had failed to live long enough to retire after sixty-five.

The massive protest politicized pensions for the first time since Drees was swept to power on the strength of his pension reforms in 1948. If pension fury continued to grow, untouchable regulators such as Witteveen could face increased political pressure. The protests and a growing national debate briefly delayed Witteveen's 2004 deadline, but it did not stop the march of pension reforms. The pension house was under construction. The end result was a more tightly regulated system that shifted defined benefits plans to a new hybrid that made benefits conditional on the financial health of each pension fund.

Under the new Dutch pension regime, regulation was handed to the country's central bank, De Nederlandsche

Bank. Early retirement benefits were virtually eliminated and the retirement age extended over time to sixty-seven years. A core feature of the new regulatory framework was a mechanism for relaxing pension commitments. Defined pension benefits were no longer fully guaranteed. Instead, pension benefits were linked to the financial performance of funds. Using what became known as a policy ladder, steps were set for shrinking benefits if prescribed funding levels were not met. When pension funds fell below a surplus funding ratio of 130 per cent, plan managers had to submit a recovery plan that could include increased contributions from employers and employees. If the surplus funding ratio fell below the minimum threshold of 105 per cent, inflation protections were suspended and the fund was given two years to return to a ratio of 130 per cent.

Other shock absorbers included a new approach to valuation discount rates – the rate that funds used to project future investment profits. New discount rates would be switched to an interest rate benchmark that tracked daily shifts in bank lending rates and credit risks. Like the Canada Pension Plan and many other pension regimes, the Dutch had been using a discount rate that assumed a real return on fund investments of 4 per cent. But critics argued it was an unreliable and often inaccurate indicator in volatile markets. To risk management experts, using the market to establish the discount rate was the perfect way to calibrate how much money would have to be stored away to pay their pension bills. To others it was a confusing and variable indicator that made it difficult to assess the system's costs and benefits. The simple pension system that Drees had designed was becoming very complicated.

Under Witteveen's new model, pensions would be pliable benefits that shrank in tough times and could be restored or expanded in boom years. Business and labour leaders understood the shift and explained the implications publicly, but the new model had so many opaque elements that it was largely ignored or misunderstood by the average Dutch pension member. Roaring stock markets further clouded the situation. Pension plans were raking in such huge investment returns in the buoyant markets in the mid-2000s that funding ratios soared, building fat fund surpluses that allowed many to restore such perks as inflation indexing. By the end of 2007, the average ratio of assets to liabilities at Dutch workplace pensions had leapt to 150 per cent from the lowly 2002 ratio of 110 per cent.[6]

The robust funding was a vindication of Witteveen's exacting new rules. At an international pension summit in Amsterdam in March 2007, the ever-vigilant regulator exhorted experts and regulators to continue fine-tuning funding and governance regulations to "increase the potential . . . efficiency and resilience of the pension systems." He drew attention to the industry's poor track record of communicating to pension members. Plans had to be more transparent and more easily understood so that employees were prepared for market shocks that could erode pension plan values, he said. "It is important for households to take this uncertainty into account," Witteveen proclaimed.[7] The regulator would not live long enough to fully appreciate the wisdom of his words. Six months later, in November, he died after a battle with cancer. A year later the Dutch retirement system would face the biggest test since its inception when the worst financial crisis in seventy years flattened markets around the globe.

❧

The Dutch are meticulous renovators. Amsterdam's palatial Rijksmuseum, which houses Rembrandt's masterpieces, reopened in April 2013 after ten years of intricate structural restorations. The nearby Van Gogh museum was back in business a month later after a year of repair. Then there's the Royal Picture Gallery Mauritshuis, home to Vermeer's fabled *Girl with a Pearl Earring* painting, set to reopen in 2014 after a two-year overhaul. What other country would have the patience to shutter popular public institutions for so long? In the Netherlands taxpayers are willing to spend time and money to properly fix institutions of vital public interest.

After the 2008 financial crisis, the Dutch approached the pension crisis with unhurried deliberation. In 2011, representatives of labour, business, and government struck an accord to overhaul the country's pension system. The contours of pension reform legislation are set to be unveiled in the summer of 2013, when the Netherland's central bank will publicly issue proposals for a new regulatory model. Labour and business groups will deliberate on and provide feedback on these proposals, leading to legislation as early as 2014.

There is little doubt the plan will transfer more retirement risks onto employees. Labour groups have reached an uneasy understanding that the country's generous retirement system is too expensive in the wake of the financial crisis and steady increases in longevity projections. The social partners have agreed to freeze future contribution hikes. Still up for discussion, however, are future benefits and funding security guidelines. The debate has frayed the ties that bind social partners. Still, as this is written, it appears labour is moving closer to conciliation and consensus. If it holds, the social partners will fully abandon the generous benefit guarantees that were the cornerstone of Willem Drees's reforms.

The rigorous funding rules that Witteveen called for in the early 2000s helped shelter pension funds from the catastrophic injuries that crippled plans in so many other countries. But the venerable Dutch system did not escape unscathed. For the first time ever, the pension system had a funding shortfall. As a consequence of investment losses and plunging real interest rates, by the end of 2008, Dutch funds had on average only 95 per cent of assets needed to cover obligations, a huge drop from the 130 per cent surplus funding ratio in 2007. More than CAN$145 billion was erased from the market value of pension assets. Taking the biggest hits was ABP, the mammoth $361 billion pension fund for Dutch civil servants and teachers. In 2008, the fund saw the value of assets plunge by 20 per cent, or $57 billion, accounting for a third of the entire country's pension losses. The wipeout left one of the world's biggest pension funds with only 89 per cent of the assets required to cover pension commitments. Evoking the falling-land crisis in medieval times, locals began calling the Dutch pension plan "the sinking giant."

Compared with pension plans in North America, where plan deficits are much larger, the Dutch shortfalls seem like a small fender bender. But in the Netherlands, where pensions are debated with the same fervour as hockey in Canada, the losses are a national disaster. For the first time since strict funding rules were set in the early 2000s, pension benefits and contributions had to be adjusted to compensate for deficits in hundreds of plans.

The Netherlands suffers from a number of the same pension ailments that weakened other regimes. Like in New Brunswick and Rhode Island, Dutch planners underestimated the financial implications of increases in retiree lifespans. Dutch pension funds also invested heavily in the stock market, leaving them vulnerable to the financial crisis. Adding to Dutch pension stress are Witteveen's rigorous funding rules: whereas injured North American plans were given a decade or more to recover funding deficits, underfunded Dutch pension funds were required to rebuild surpluses within a few years. Adding further pressure was the market rate used by funds to estimate what assets they would need to pay pension bills. After the crash, market rates collapsed, forcing pension plans to either accumulate more assets or reduce pension benefits.

If there was any pension complacency in the Netherlands, it evaporated by 2011. The recovery plan that followed the financial crisis forced pension plan members to finally confront the enormous costs of preserving the nation's magnanimous retirement system.

For the first time since the system of adjustable benefits was introduced in the early 2000s, the vast majority of pension plans had to trim benefits to comply with funding rules. Meanwhile, pension contribution rates rose sharply, costing plan members between 15 per cent and 20 per cent of their paycheques by 2013. The new rates were so unpopular that the last day of the workweek became known as "pension Friday" in the Netherlands because anyone paying a contribution rate near 20 per cent was giving up the equivalent of a day's earnings. Employers also paid heavily. In 2009, Royal Dutch Shell pumped CAN$2.6 billion into its $25 billion pension fund to restore its surplus. The oil and gas giant estimated that the one-time injection was more than twice the fixed annual salaries earned by its pension plan members.

The biggest shock was benefit reductions. Following the crash of 2008, an estimated 80 per cent of the country's pension funds fell below the minimum surplus threshold of 105 per cent. The plunge activated a funding rule that forced plans to suspend benefits such as inflation protections. When the deadline arrived in the spring of 2013, more than sixty funds had to further reduce pension benefits including, in some cases, pension income. The Netherlands' central bank does not disclose the identity of the pension plans or details of the cuts other than to say the average benefit cut was nearly 2 per cent. The setback affected 3 million workers and retirees.

Dutch workers initially responded to pension turmoil with protests and work stoppages in 2009, but outbursts were smaller than the massive demonstration of 2004. Surveys revealed widespread confusion about pension cuts. One survey showed that nearly 70 per cent of respondents believed they were receiving smaller pensions because 30 per cent of their contributions paid for fund expenses.[8] A Netherlands' central bank study, however, said costs only amounted to 3.5 per cent of member contributions. The Dutch have more than a funding issue; they have a communication problem. The pension system has evolved into such a complex machine with adjustable parts and variable rates that it is almost impossible for the average member to understand. The financial crisis and pension confusion has sent the country's retirement designers back to the drawing board. Since the pension accord of 2011, labour, business, and government experts have debated a variety of new models. As of the summer of 2013, business and labour support was growing for a new hybrid plan that, alas, was anything but simple.

Chris Driessen, an Amsterdam-based economist with the giant FNV confederation of trade unions, has been advising members for three decades on pension benefits. He does not talk about injustices or broken contracts when he discusses the country's move away from secure defined benefits. Those days, he concedes, are gone.

"Now everyone agrees that the guarantees in the old system are no longer possible," he said. The problem with the current regime, Driessen believes, is that it places too much emphasis on security. Members are paying so much in pension contributions that employees are starting to balk. "Some of our younger workers are threatening to leave their plans and create individual defined contribution plans," he said.

To prevent the exodus, he advocates relaxing Witteveen's funding rules. He believes the system is strong enough to ease away from the strict funding rules and low discount-rate benchmark. Labour complaints have found a sympathetic ear with some businesses. Royal Dutch Shell and other major employers have been vocal about the unpredictable and heavy costs of current funding standards. To ease the burden, some businesses and labour groups are advocating a new "defined ambition" pension model. This pension concept is more than a push away from strict funding rules – it is an acknowledgement that pension guarantees are no longer sustainable.

A leading advocate of the new pension hybrid is Niels Kortleve, a manager with PGGM, a pension service company to Dutch employers. Kortleve's job description at PGGM is "innovator," and his office is located in an airy new glass-and-steel complex surrounded by horse fields near the town of Zeist. In this bucolic setting, Kortleve talks of a new pension world in which the Netherlands moves to what he calls a "softer" hybrid. In the defined ambition model, traditional Dutch pension guarantees are replaced with benefit targets. These ambitions would be easier to achieve under the proposed model because funding rules are relaxed. Pension plans would no longer be required to reserve a surplus to cushion against market shocks. When asset values fall below pension obligations, plans are required to eliminate the shortfall through annual benefit cuts. The impact of these losses would be softened by stretching the cuts over a ten-year period. The discount rate under this system is also more generous. It allows plans to move away from current market rates to a more theoretical rate that is custom-designed by each plan according to estimated longevity rates for plan members and future pension obligations. This approach offers less-certain benefits, concedes Kortleve, but eliminates the heavy yoke of "unsustainable pension promises." He calls the defined ambition a "sustainability instrument" that gives plans the flexibility to lower benefits when market or demographic shocks threaten funding.

The defined ambition plan has many critics. One of the most vocal is a Rotterdam-based pension consultant who spends his spare time producing satirical videos about market and debt crises with Monty Python founder Terry Jones. Theo Kocken's first film, *Risky Business and the Business of Risk*, featured a vintage Monty Python skit about raging, purse-swinging grannies as a way of warning viewers about the burden of supporting greying populations. These days, Kocken is taking swings at promoters of the defined ambition pension model. He says the plan is so complex "it will confuse 99 per cent of the people." He also warns it is potentially reckless because it relies on a subjective discount rate that "is prone to manipulation." If funds are too optimistic with their investment projections, "they will pay too much to retirees, leaving insufficient assets for younger generations."

Kocken is a risk management specialist whose company, Cordano Group, advises pension plans on how to mitigate market shocks through a variety of financial instruments such as derivative contracts. As the Netherlands moves away from traditional pension guarantees, he advocates a two-part approach conceived by Toronto pension consultant Keith Ambachtsheer. Under this model, the Netherlands would stick with its current funding rules. Pension benefits would no longer be guaranteed, but retirees could have more certainty about a large share of their income by allocating some pension investments to conservative products such as annuities that pay fixed amounts at a set date. "The old model promised too much, the new defined ambition model promises nothing," Kocken said. "The optimal system should be something in between."

Dirk Broeders glides through a warren of hallways and meeting rooms housed within De Nederlandsche Bank's Amsterdam glass-and-steel fortress, talking easily about the Dutch pension system. Lean and athletic, his tanned face is framed by short dark hair and thick black glasses. Seated finally in a boardroom, Broeders's sun-darkened face goes pale, however, when asked what his late boss, Dirk Witteveen, might think about the current state of Dutch pensions.

"In its current form our system is not sustainable because of the costs of longer life expectancies," he said. "Ultimately we have to talk about lower benefits."

Broeders is feeling the weight of the Netherlands' pension challenges. He has been handed the burden of drafting government proposals for new pension models, which are due to be released in the summer of 2013. Although he is restricted from discussing details of the changes, Broeders concedes they will be "controversial." Historically, Dutch politicians have given pension regulators a wide berth. But in the wake of the financial crisis and pension cuts, the retirement system has become the subject of national debate. Everyone from taxi drivers to politicians has an opinion about how the pension system should be fixed. In such a contentious environment, the Netherlands is moving to a compromise to secure the support of business and labour social partners.

The compromise is expected to be a choice between two pension models. One could permit pension plans to stay within a re-engineered version of the current regime, allowing for some benefits to be guaranteed when the fund has a surplus. The other could be one of two potential models. One might be a variation on the complex defined ambition, or "real," model backed by Kortleve and other unions. Another could be the two-part plan backed by Kocken and others that would allow a portion of pension benefits to be preserved with an annuity purchase.

Regardless of which approach is chosen, few disagree that the world's most admired pension system is undergoing significant renovations. As a result of market shocks and increased life expectancy rates, the Netherlands has come to understand that the long-term costs of pension guarantees envisioned by Father Drees are too onerous.

To secure the long-term future of a system that promises pensions to more than 90 per cent of the country's workers, pensions are becoming adjustable benefits that shrink or expand in relation to market swings and life expectancy. Calibrating the right balance won't be easy, said Broeders, because the future of the system is at stake.

"If you get the design wrong," he said, "you can really damage the retirements of the younger generation."

CHAPTER 5

SOLVING CANADA'S PENSION CRISIS

The Golden Fish

There is a modern variation of an old Russian folk tale that neatly captures the social context of our ripening pension crisis:

> Distraught over the loss of his most productive cow, a farmer grabs his fishing pole and sets out for a nearby stream. Sitting by a gurgling brook, the farmer jerks to attention when the wood rod bends in his hands. Acting quickly, he pulls in his line to discover a large golden creature – a magic fish. As he pulls his catch closer, the creature begins to speak.

> "Please, sir, I am a magic fish. Let me go and I will grant you any wish."
>
> The startled farmer's eyes narrow in suspicion.
>
> "Anything you desire," the golden fish again promises.
>
> The farmer considers the unusual offer for some time. And then a smile crosses his face. "Anything?" he asks.
>
> "Anything," the fish agrees.
>
> "All right then, I want my neighbour's cow to die!"

And so we have the social dynamic of the pension debate. In Canada and the United States, where a majority of employees do not have workplace pensions, the call for reform is often shaped by envy, anger, and fear. Some want to end the disparity by killing what they view to be "gold-plated" pensions that sustain others. Older workers cling to costly benefits that endanger the next generation's pensions. Young workers balk at increasingly expensive contributions for pensions they fear they will never see. Shareholders pressure companies to limit pension costs. Small businesses reject basic pension plans for employees. A majority of Canadians are not saving enough to sustain their lifestyles through retirement. Politicians choose cutting public services over repairing unsustainable pension plans. Unions exhort members to cling to retirement benefits that threaten pension viability.

While the debate escalates, gaps in our pension system grow wider. Today, more than 60 per cent of employed Canadians do not have a workplace pension, and most in this group lack sufficient savings to support their lifestyles in retirement. The remaining employees have pensions, but these plans are either insufficient or endangered by demographic and market upheavals that plan designers never imagined. This shouldn't be news. Our pension crisis was predicted years ago by academics, actuaries, labour groups, consultants, and financial institutions. In the past six years alone, the pension challenge has been studied by four provincial commissions: a joint panel involving representatives from British Columbia and Alberta has been heard from; Ontario, Quebec, and Nova Scotia have also weighed in with expert committee findings.

Few of the substantive recommendations from these commissions have been implemented. Our problem is not a shortage of ideas but rather a lack of courage and political will. Canada's last major pension initiative was the introduction of Old Age Security (OAS), Guaranteed Income Supplement (GIC), the Canada Pension Plan (CPP), and the Quebec Pension Plan (QPP). These programs earned Canada global recognition for low senior poverty rates. These reforms, however, are more than forty years old. Overlooked is a growing majority of Canadians who have no workplace pensions. Then there are those with inadequate pension plans or those whose plans are threatened by market volatility or longevity risks. If nothing changes, it is possible, indeed probable, that all taxpayers will find themselves burdened with the expense of rescuing and providing for a generation of marooned, financially unprotected retirees. Government, labour, and business leaders are so worried about the infamous third rail that they don't see the runaway train hurtling our way. We believe this train can be stopped. If we act now, the healthiest parts of our pension system can be redesigned and more effective retirement savings options created. Some of these innovations are being tested in our own backyard in New Brunswick and farther afield in Rhode Island and the Netherlands. These early reforms are creating more resilient and flexible pension models that can adjust to modern challenges. If we have learned anything from reforms in New Brunswick, Rhode Island, and the Netherlands, it is that indifference and neglect is the enemy of crumbling retirement systems.

Without the discipline of clear funding rules, Rhode Island turned a blind eye to perilously underfunded public sector pension plans until municipal governments failed and essential services were cut. When a reform-minded treasurer and newly elected municipal leaders finally took action, there was so little money left to repair the damage that some retirees lost as much as 50 per cent of their benefits. New Brunswick was nimble enough to push for change before some of its biggest pension plans imploded. With the help of pragmatic union leaders and a nervy premier, the province introduced innovative laws that have to date given half-a-dozen public and private sector pension plans a new life. In contrast, the Netherlands imposed strict funding rules after the dot-com crash, allowing the country's pension system to survive the 2008 financial crisis in better shape than most other retirement systems. Its head start in the early 2000s gave the country the time and the resources to once again push for difficult and controversial new rules after the crash exposed that even this globally admired pension system had frailties.

Dutch innovations have shaped pension reforms in New Brunswick and Rhode Island and are proposed as a solution to some of Britain's pension woes. At the heart of the Dutch model is a new mindset that all pension benefits can no longer be 100 per cent guaranteed. In a world where investment returns are projected to remain unusually low and volatile and where retirement years will soon be longer than career years, fully guaranteed pension benefits are endangering the very future of pensions themselves. As Rhode Island treasurer Gina Raimondo put it so bluntly in her *Truth in Numbers* report, the traditional defined benefit pension no longer adds up. Unless employees and employers are willing to agree to sharp increases in their pension contributions, the best alternative is a reform model that calls for a set of benefits that adjusts to market and longevity shifts.

In Rhode Island, New Brunswick, and the Netherlands, the shifts to new pension regimes are in their early fragile days. Each jurisdiction faces legal and political challenges that, as of this writing, have not deterred reform champions. Canada's pension system may not be as robust as the Netherlands, but neither is it as desperate as Rhode Island or New Brunswick. If we wait too long, like Rhode Island, to redesign a pension system that is at risk, workers, retirees, and taxpayers (that is to say, everybody) will pay heavily. If we act now, we can build on our strengths by redesigning existing pensions, eliminating counter-productive regulatory and tax rules, and opening new pension opportunities.

Some political leaders dispute the need for pension reform. After all, the Organisation for Economic Cooperation and Development (OECD) ranks our elderly poverty rates among the lowest in the world, and the Melbourne Mercer Global Pension Index ranks our pension regime as the sixth best of seventeen countries surveyed. But closer scrutiny of these surveys reveals fault lines. When the sustainability of our pension system is ranked, we fall to eighth place. This lower rating tells us we are headed for trouble. Why? Because most Canadians haven't saved enough for retirement and the majority of our pension plans use outdated investment and mortality assumptions that understate market and longevity threats that jeopardize our pensions. The time to take action is now. It is beyond the scope of this book to provide a comprehensive solution for a pension system governed by a web of federal and provincial legislation, tax, accounting, labour, and corporate laws. We do believe, however, that there are a number of effective and affordable proposals that offer valuable solutions to our most urgent pension problems: a stronger safety net for millions of workers who do not have workplace pensions and more sustainable and effective pensions for those that do.

Before any of these innovations can be discussed, it is important to review how Canada's retirement system works.

Canada's Pillars

Canada's pension system can be thought of as a house where new floors are added every year to accommodate an inflow of retirees who increasingly outnumber those that pass away. As more residents flood in every year, little is done to reinforce the three pillars that are groaning under the weight of this growing burden.

The first pillar is the nation's strongest. It offers a mix of government-funded supplements that are designed to keep elderly incomes above the poverty line. Reforms initiated by Ottawa in the 1960s have been so successful that Canada now has one of the lowest senior poverty rates in the world. The centrepieces of the federal program are the Old Age Security (OAS) and Guaranteed Income Supplement (GIS). Eligible Canadian residents can receive up to about $6,500 annually in OAS payments starting at the age of sixty-five. These payments, depending on the retiree's income, can be supplemented with GIS benefits of as much as $8,800 annually. Unlike the simple Dutch pension scheme, which pays all residents the same flat rate, Canada's first-pillar pensions are subject to a variety of complex adjustments that allow Ottawa to clawback GIS payments if retirees' income exceeds certain thresholds.

The second pillar is made up of compulsory, government-sponsored workplace pension plans that are financed with contributions from employers, employees, and the self-employed. Quebec has the QPP; the rest of the country has the CPP. These plans are designed to create a basic income for retired workers. The maximum pension is equal to approximately 25 per cent of the country's average wage, handing eligible retirees up to about $12,150 annually.

The combination of pillar-one OAS and GIS supplements and pillar-two government sponsored workplace pensions means that a typical elderly retiree with no other income receives $15,300 as of 2013, while couples receive up to $28,000, with adjustments for inflation. These two pillars ensure that couples earning less than $30,000 in wages will see most of their pre-tax income replaced by the first two pension pillars during retirement. For workers earning more than $30,000 and less than $100,000, which means most Canadians, income replacement is a much more significant challenge. To avoid a sharp drop in lifestyles, these retirees will have to set aside a larger share of their income for pension or other savings plans that are increasingly scarce, risky, or expensive.

The third pillar is Canada's shakiest. It is made up of workplace- and union-sponsored pensions and registered retirement savings plans (RRSPs). About 38 per cent of the country's 19 million workers are enrolled in pension plans. About a third, or nearly 5 million workers, are members of defined benefit plans. The good news about defined benefit plans is that they are the most reliable and cost-effective retirement saving vehicles available in Canada. The majority of assets held by these defined benefit plans are pooled in a handful of large funds that are admired globally for their innovative and successful investment strategies. However, there are a large number of small defined benefit plans that cannot realize the benefits of scale enjoyed by bigger funds.

The bad news about our defined benefit success is that today the vast majority of the benefits are available only to Canadian workers employed by deep-pocketed governments or, to a lesser extent, major companies. Since the 1970s, the percentage of private sector employees enrolled in defined benefit plans has shrunk to 12 per cent from about 35 per cent. The decline is partly explained by the erosion of Canada's manufacturing belt, which traditionally paid defined benefits as part of contracts negotiated during collective bargaining with unions. Funding challenges and increased shareholder scrutiny also contributed to the retreat. Pension funds have shifted their investments increasingly to volatile stock investments to compensate for falling rates on traditional fixed investments such as bonds. The shift exposed pension funds to two of the worst equity collapses of the century, the dot-com crash in 2001 and the financial crisis of 2008. The wipeouts left pension funds with huge deficits just as retiring baby boom workers were beginning to strain the system.

Until the mid-1980s, publicly listed companies seldom disclosed details of their sponsored plans. That changed in 1985 when the first of a series of accounting standard changes forced companies to disclose the status of their pension funding. Increased public scrutiny, coupled with tightened accounting rules, complex and inconsistent provincial regulations, and uncertainty about the ownership of fund surpluses discouraged corporate sponsorship of defined benefit pension plans. Today, only one-quarter of private sector employees have pensions; the vast majority of these are defined contribution plans, which are riskier for plan members. Under these plans, employees and employers, if they choose, make contributions to accounts set up for individual workers. The cost of managing the investments is high, and retirement benefits are determined by investment gains or losses.

A growing number of companies are freezing existing defined benefit plans and offering new employees an array of defined contribution plans. These plans are more confusing, expensive, and less reliable, leading in most cases to inadequate pensions. Companies typically require employees, many of whom have limited financial expertise, to select their individual pension savings program from a bewildering array of investment options. Few workers entering the workforce have sufficient interest or the financial wisdom to save for their days as an old person. If the transition to defined contribution plans continues, then the major pension funds that manage hundreds of billions of dollars of Canadian pension savings will increasingly be splintered into millions of small, individual plans that are far riskier and more expensive.

Registered retirement savings plans (RRSPs) have failed their initial promise in the 1950s to finance retirement dreams. Since these savings plans are voluntary, only a third of Canadian workers participate in them. Paradoxically the most active RRSP investors are employees with workplace pensions. About half of Canadian employees who belong to pension plans also invest in RRSPs, yet only about a quarter of those *without* pensions invest in these personal savings plans.[1] Employees without pensions typically earn lower incomes, leaving them with less money to invest. One conclusion we have drawn from these low participation rates is that voluntary savings schemes are not effective. The same would hold true for the recently introduced tax-free savings account (TFSA). The limited reach, coupled with high fees and flat returns, have prompted Canadians to question the value of any of these voluntary savings plans.

As the third pillar continues to weaken, the pension burden is falling increasingly to the first pillar: federally financed supplements for the elderly. It is a load that will eventually prove too onerous. OAS and GIS are already the nation's largest fiscal expense, and the annual cost is projected to triple to $108 billion by 2030. We can choose to pay an ever-increasing tax bill. Or we can redesign workplace pensions and employee retirement investment programs to broaden the safety net with a more efficient, flexible, and viable retirement system.

Saving the Forgotten Middle

If there was a triage ward for workers facing acute retirement income failure, it would be filled with middle-income employees without workplace pensions. More than 5 million Canadian workers with incomes ranging from $30,000 to $100,000 have no workplace pension. Most lack the resources, expertise, and discipline to save enough or invest effectively to maintain their lifestyle in retirement. A recent study estimates workers must save between 10 per cent and 21 per cent of pre-tax earnings for thirty-five years to replace 70 per cent of working wages.[2] Given that Canada's saving rate has plunged to a scant 5.5 per cent from 20 per cent in the early 1980s, it's a safe bet that few of these middle-income earners have sufficient retirement savings.

The Canada Pension Plan (CPP) will be of marginal assistance to middle-income earners because the current annual pension limit of $12,150 only replaces a fraction of most salaries in this group. Employees earning less than $30,000 will be much better off in retirement because the combination of CPP and the federal government's

OAS and GIS provides them an annual income that virtually replaces pre-retirement wages, after tax.

Middle-income workers seldom get attention in the pension debate because anyone earning between $30,000 and $100,000 is presumed to be self-sufficient. If they haven't saved enough they have only themselves to blame, or so the debate goes. There are no shortage of finger-wagging bloggers and financial advisers exhorting Canadians to save for their golden years. The more advice we get, however, the less we seem to save. For a variety of financial and behavioural reasons, as demonstrated by the failure of RRSPs, voluntary savings plans aren't going to solve the looming income crunch for pension-less, middle-income workers. When this vast demographic leaves work, their vertiginous income drop will have enormous repercussions for the consumer sector, government tax revenues, and the cost of federal old age supplements.

Fixing this problem shouldn't be difficult. One compelling proposal could be launched quickly by taking advantage of existing pension infrastructure. This approach calls for an expansion of CPP benefits to bridge the pension vacuum for middle-income earners. Various proposals have been studied by a variety of pension experts, most recently Bob Baldwin, an Ottawa pension consultant. Under this model, middle-income earners without workplace pensions would receive a larger CPP pension.[3] At present, an employee taking home a $50,000 salary receives a maximum CPP pension of $12,150 annually if they retire at sixty-five after thirty-nine years of work. In addition, this worker is eligible for a $6,552 OAS supplement. The annual retirement income adds up to $18,700, replacing only 37 per cent of the salary.

The enhanced model offers an affordable solution to the retirement crunch. One scenario gives the biggest CPP boost to the middle of the middle-income group, the $50,000 wage earner. These enhancements would be financed with increased contributions. For example, employees earning $50,000 a year would increase their regular contributions to CPP annually to $2,930 from the current $2,300. Employers would match the contribution hike. The bigger contributions would allow those earning $50,000 to increase their CPP pension to $17,500. Add OAS payments and the total retirement income rises to $24,050, replacing nearly half of a worker's salary. An employee earning $100,000 would see CPP and OAS income jump to $37,000. (See chart, page 150)

This approach is not without obstacles. Currently CPP is not a fully pre-funded pension plan like a defined benefit plan. It is a "pay-as-you-go-plan," which means a large portion of today's contributions are directed to pay the pensions of retired members. To accommodate the

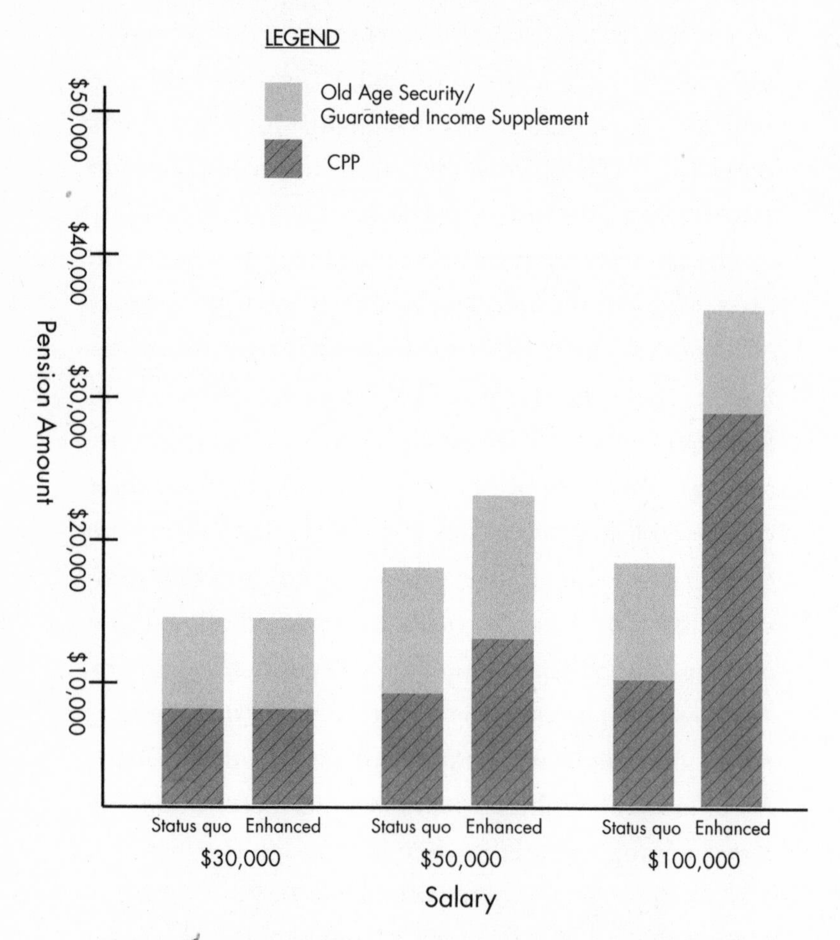

Status quo CPP – assumes that CPP is earned at the rate of 25% on earnings up to $50,000 (2013 maximum earnings threshold is $48,600).

Enhanced CPP proposal – assumes that CPP is earned at the rate of 25% on earnings up to $30,000; 50% on earnings from $30,000 to $50,000; and 25% on earnings from $50,000 to a maximum of $100,000.

expanded CPP pension, it may be necessary to create a separate investment board to manage the additional contributions. The challenges of expanding CPP are very real, but they are manageable. To date, the federal government has ignored any proposal to expand CPP. Vocal opposition from the Canadian Federation of Independent Business may explain government inaction.

The lobby group warned in a June 2013 statement that even a modest improvement in CPP contributions by small business employers would be such a financial strain that it would cost seven hundred thousand person years of employment over twenty years. The reality is, however, that this scary scenario has little application to the enhanced CPP contributions for middle-income earners. The biggest contribution hikes for employers in the proposed scheme affects workers earning $50,000 or more. These salary levels exceed the average $40,000 income earned by Canadian employees working for a business with less than one hundred workers, according to Statistics Canada. In addition, this enhancement to CPP benefits could be fully integrated with any existing workplace pension so, in these cases, there would be no net increase in contribution cost for the employee and employer.

There is also the issue of time. Supporters of the enhanced CPP benefits argue it should be fully funded by contributions throughout an employee's career before the increase takes effect. This means the first fully enhanced pension would not be paid until after 2050, long after baby boomers have retired. Ottawa could consider speeding up the delivery of enhanced pensions by temporarily bridging the gap to fully fund the new benefits. Ottawa and Quebec initially funded CPP and QPP pensions when they were introduced in the 1960s, an approach that saw retirees receive the first full pensions within a decade. A portion of this cost would be offset by reduced federal OAS and GIS payments.

Redefining Defined Benefits

Canada has a big advantage over most pension-challenged regimes. A greater percentage of defined benefit plans are offered to Canadian workers than to their counterparts in Australia, the United States, and Britain. According to the OECD, Canada's ratio of defined benefit plans to total pension assets ranks as the world's fourth largest behind Germany, Norway, and Finland.[4] Some would suggest this statistic signals Canada is behind the times. Other countries are jettisoning defined benefit plans because they are perceived to have become too much of a burden for sponsoring governments and companies. Canada, it is said, should follow the trend.

We believe this approach is misguided. To be sure, the traditional defined benefit pension model needs to be more flexible to adjust to unpredictable modern challenges. But this does not mean we should toss it on the scrap heap. Workers and retirees who contribute to and collect pensions from Canada's giant public sector pension funds have created a unique national asset. Nearly 6 million workers and more than 3 million retirees currently belong to public sector defined benefit plans. These plans compel employees to set aside an average of about one-tenth of their pay for pension savings, which in addition to employer contributions adds up to nearly $50 billion annually. The savings are managed by large funds that oversee more than half a trillion dollars of assets.

By almost any measure our defined benefit pensions are the most effective retirement savings system in the country. As an expert committee on the Future of the Quebec retirement system said in a 2013 report: "Defined benefit plans provide the type of financial security that should be emphasized. . . . No other supplemental pension plans or personal savings vehicles can provide members with the same level of financial security."

Savings are pooled in large funds that have the scale to keep management costs low. They have the financial heft to invest money in higher-yielding big investments such as real estate and infrastructure. Size allows funds to disperse pension investment risks among a broad membership. And it cushions individuals against the risks of running out of pension savings if their retirement extends longer than expected. To put it bluntly, the cost of supporting those retirees who live longer than average will be balanced by those who don't. These factors in aggregate make the defined benefit model the least expensive pension plan option.

Retirees with defined benefit pensions are an important economic force in Canada. They spend an estimated $60 billion on real estate, consumer goods, and services annually. Another $13 billion is paid annually in income, sales, and real estate taxes. They are so self-sufficient that only an estimated 20 per cent of retirees with defined benefits are eligible for federal GIS supplements. In contrast, nearly 40 per cent of retirees without defined benefits receive the government supplements.[5] Any government money that would be saved reducing defined benefit plans would likely later be spent on larger GIS payments. Killing successful existing pension programs would be like robbing Peter to pay Paul, then having to repay Peter twenty years down the line.

Canada's top ten public sector pension funds manage more than $750 billion, or 35 per cent, of all Canadian retirement assets. They are: the Canada Pension Plan Investment Board, Caisse de dépôt et placement du Québec, Ontario Teachers' Pension Plan Board, British

Columbia Investment Management Corp., Public Sector Pension Investment Board, Ontario Municipal Employees Retirement System, Healthcare of Ontario Pension Plan, Alberta Investment Management Corp., Ontario Pension Board, and OPSEU Pension Trust. The funds are long-term investors that own the stocks and bonds of Canadian and foreign businesses, operating everything from shopping malls to tollways.

The advantages of large funds are investment efficiency and expertise. Defined benefit plans cost much less to operate because individual savings are pooled in large funds, giving them the scale to lower members' administrative and investment expenses. According to Alicia Munnell, a Boston College economist and pension authority, the operating costs of managing individual defined contribution plans in the United States are more than twice those of defined benefit plans.[6] In Canada, the cost disadvantage is much greater because fees charged by mutual funds, a common investment choice for defined contribution plans, rank among the highest in the world, costing more than twice those in the United States. Larger funds also tend to have significantly better investment track records than individual retirement plans.

Shifting Canada's defined benefit pensions to defined contribution plans is no solution to our retirement savings crisis. Followed to its logical conclusion, it would replace a mandatory and efficient fund regime with a fragmented, non-compulsory, expensive, and risky savings system that would leave retirees with less income. The loss of defined benefits would also spell the erosion of the large pension plans that supply so much of Canada's long-term capital. This strategy saves us nothing in the long run. In fact, the Canadian taxpayer and the economy will end up paying more. There is a better future for defined benefit plans. The first priority is a new approach to how we regulate, govern, and tailor defined benefits. The ultimate goal is to ensure plans have the flexibility to adapt to volatile and unpredictable market and demographic forces. The second is to encourage the consolidation of a highly fragmented fund landscape. The third challenge would be redesigning the pension framework so that one of Canada's most important savings pools is more prudently and effectively governed. Many players need to come to the table to make these reforms possible. We need governments to back new laws, a stronger regulator focused on pension funding risks, employees and pensioners to share more of the risks, and labour leaders to set more realistic pension expectations.

New Brunswick and Rhode Island are North America's pension reform pioneers because the challenges that all defined benefit plans face happened faster in these regimes because of poor pension oversight; benefit excesses and funding failures left their retirement systems more vulnerable to financial storms. They moved first because the alternative was widespread pension failures. The rest of Canada's defined benefit plans don't face the same immediate threats, but over the next decades the combination of retiring baby boomers, low returns, and volatile markets will impose the same unbearable strains on traditional defined benefit plans. They simply weren't constructed to absorb these shocks.

As the number of baby boom retirees continues to rise it will only be a matter of time before they outnumber working members. This means that net cash outflow (benefits paid to retirees less contributions received) from these maturing pension funds will continue to increase. This is not a problem as long as funds continue to generate investment returns. But should another dot-com crash or 2008 financial crisis hit our pension system as it is currently constructed, the consequences will eventually be borne by younger plan members. They will be faced with increasing contributions or cutting future benefits to protect benefits paid to retirees. In this scenario, younger workers will understandably begin to question the value of pension plans. We can wait until we reach this tipping point or act now to ensure more pension security while providing a better, fairer deal for our children.

The Dutch offer the most pragmatic solution to the defined benefit challenge. One of the world's most admired retirement systems moved to a new model in the mid-2000s after labour and corporate leaders agreed with regulators that fully guaranteed benefits were no longer possible. The best possible solution was for plan members to share additional funding risks with employers. As a result, the traditional notion of a fully guaranteed pension has been replaced by a more conditional plan linking benefits to the investment performance of pension plans. The most flexible benefit in this model is inflation adjustments embedded in pension benefits. If plans experience funding shortfalls, inflation-indexed pension benefits are suspended until surpluses are restored. This approach creates a simple and fair lever for managing funding challenges.

There are a number of different methods for adjusting inflation benefits. British Columbia, for example, converted inflation adjustments into a conditional benefit in 1982 for some of its public sector plans when the province became concerned about double-digit inflation. Under the B.C. model, inflation indexation is treated as a separate benefit tier that is only paid if pension funds have sufficient assets. More recently, one public sector plan in the province set a cap of 1.83 per cent on inflation adjustments. Another has deferred inflation adjustments for employees who take early retirement.

Other Dutch solutions include increased pension contributions by workers and, if pension deficits are severe, cuts in retirees' base pensions. When these changes were introduced in the mid-2000s, they elicited little response from employees and pensioners. When the cuts took effect after the 2008 financial crisis, however, politicians, labour leaders, and employers in the Netherlands were confronted with an angry rebellion from workers who had not fully grasped the significance of the changes.

The outburst underlines the importance of clear and transparent communication regarding pension changes. Rhode Island treasurer Gina Raimondo understood the importance of getting the message out in publicizing her *Truth in Numbers* report in her own state. She personally took her pension reform message to hundreds of plan members and retirees, winning widespread political support for legislation that includes conditional retirement benefits such as inflation indexing. New Brunswick hired pension experts to personally explain changes to reluctant plan members and labour leaders. It has been an uphill battle, but if a recent commentary in Saint John's *Telegraph-Journal* from retired New Brunswick Power economist Michael Wong is any indication, government workers are coming to a new understanding about the pension contract:

> We, the cohort of retirees, like to say that we earned all of the benefits . . . guaranteed full indexation included; and, in part, we did. But when we started our public service career in 1975, we had not contracted nor paid for the longevity benefits that we are, and will continue to be enjoying many years into the future. Perhaps it's time to pay it forward—through conditional indexation that applies to all.[7]

Recent pension reforms should be seen as building blocks for a smarter retirement system. Always we should strive to understand we are not planning for pensions but for people. The takeaway from early battles for pension reform in North America and the Netherlands is that frightened people resist change. It may be possible to alleviate retiree stress about conditional benefits by preserving retirees' base pensions through an insurance product known as an annuity that pays a fixed income to retirees. This annuity could be provided by an insurance company or by a separate division of the pension plan. Another option is linking pension plan retirement ages to longevity forecasts for the plan's membership. When lifespan projections are increased, retirement ages or benefit payments can be delayed.

In an environment where markets and demographics are much more volatile, our notion of pension security is shifting. Until recently most employees equated the security of their pension plan with the financial health of their employer. As long as the organization was making money, it was assumed, pension benefits would be paid. Years of market and corporate failures have shown us the unreliability of that assumption. Today the best pension insurance is a tight risk management policy that ensures, among other things, that a fund always has the protective cushion of a surplus. Greater pension security can also be achieved by streamlining pension funds. The fragmentation of defined benefit savings plans is a wasted opportunity to reduce management fees and spread investment and longevity risks among larger plan memberships that share similar demographic profiles. Defined benefit pension savings, largely managed by public sector plans, are divided among hundreds of provincial and municipal funds. In Ontario, for example, there are one hundred public sector pension funds each with their own investment and administrative staff. About 75 per cent of the funds are so small that they each manage less than $1 billion of assets. A report to the Ontario government by pension adviser William Morneau estimated public sector funds could save $75 million annually by pooling smaller funds under the administration of a new asset manager.[8] The consolidation of pension savings would also give funds the heft to invest in higher returning asset classes such as large real estate or infrastructure projects.

The long-term goal of these proposals is a flexible pension system that can continue to adapt to unpredictable market and longevity trends. Such a program is not sustainable unless everyone shares the costs and rewards of conditional benefits. We are recommending a model that is more intricate than the long-standing defined benefit plan. It calls for rigorous governance and regulation. Canada could learn from Willem Drees's visionary move in the 1950s to transfer oversight of the Netherlands' pension plans to independent trusts with boards appointed by employees and employers. Similarly Ontario has a class of public sector funds, known as jointly sponsored pension plans, which are jointly governed by employees and employers. These funds include the Ontario Teachers' Pension Plan Board, Ontario Municipal Employees Retirement System, and Healthcare of Ontario Pension Plan. The model should be extended to other pension plans to shield pension savings from political and corporate interference. It would also make directors duty-bound by law to act in the plan's long-term best interests.

As we have seen in Rhode Island and New Brunswick, the long-term needs of pension savings can be subverted by short-term needs of political, business, and labour agendas. Pension benefits are routinely negotiated during the push–pull of collective bargaining for short-term contracts. It makes no sense to put our economy's future in the hands of individuals who are judged by short-term results or contracts. Pension benefit, contribution, and funding decisions belong to boards of independent and professional directors – groups that are jointly appointed by employees, retirees, and employers. These boards should be responsible for creating a funding management policy that would always think and plan in the future tense, targeting appropriate contribution rates and benefit levels. They would also be responsible for communicating the funding status and outlook for pension benefits. If employees are going to share pension risks, to contribute to help plan for their own futures, they need to understand what they're talking about.

Defined Contribution Plans that Work

Defined contribution pension plans are rapidly replacing defined benefit schemes as the corporate-sponsored pension of choice in many industrialized countries. These plans are seen as being much less onerous for employers because they are only on the hook to pay contributions, if they so choose, to individual staff pension accounts. The retreat is leaving employees, however, with risky, expensive, and unpredictable pensions. It is often left to financially inexperienced workers to select investment options, pay expensive management fees, and assume the risks of saving enough for a retirement span that is impossible to predict. Although we cannot turn the clock back on this erosion, there are a number of options for creating sturdier defined contribution plans. In the United States, so many businesses and heavily indebted state and local governments have closed defined benefit plans to new employees that defined contribution schemes now account for 50 per cent of the country's pension plans. The level is nearly 40 per cent in the United Kingdom and nearly 100 per cent in Australia. The numbers are substantially smaller in Canada, where 15 per cent of workers belong to defined contribution plans. We believe the small ratio of these plans in Canada is an opportunity. Other countries are paying heavily to fix the pension gap left by inadequate defined contribution or other retirement savings plans. The bill will be smaller in Canada.

Australia and, more recently, the United Kingdom have unveiled a number of reforms, including the creation of nationwide defined contribution pension plans for those who are not currently covered by a workplace pension. Australia started introducing these changes in the 1990s. The United Kingdom started phasing in its reforms last year to protect more than 8 million workers who either have no pensions or inadequate defined contribution plans. New mandatory contribution rules in the United Kingdom, coupled with the launch of a new national fund, are expected to cost employer and employees more than CAN$14 billion annually in additional pension contributions. If Canada followed these reforms, the bill would be significantly smaller because only 970,000 workers are currently enrolled in defined contribution plans. (As we previously recommended, middle-income workers without pensions are better served by an enhanced Canada Pension Plan, which could be integrated into existing defined benefit or defined contribution plans.)

Australia began reforming its pension system in the 1990s by requiring all employers to make fixed contributions to defined contribution pensions for employees. Using a so-called "nudge" strategy to encourage retirement savings, workers are automatically enrolled in pension plans. Workers can opt out from the plans, but the automatic enrolment is so successful that today more than three-quarters of enrolled members remain in plans. Reforms have encouraged defined contribution plan members to transfer their pension savings to larger, independent funds that charge smaller management fees and generate higher returns. The changes have reduced the number of funds today to four hundred, a huge transition from the fragmented, more costly system of forty-seven hundred funds in 1996.

The United Kingdom has borrowed from Australia and the Netherlands for recent reforms designed to assist workers with insufficient retirement savings. As of late 2012, all employers are required to begin a multi-year process of enrolling employees in pension plans. If company pension funds do not meet certain standards, employee pension savings are transferred to a separate trust known as National Employment Savings Trust (NEST). NEST operates like a giant defined contribution plan that takes regular contributions and pays pension incomes that are linked to its investment performance. Unlike small, individual defined contribution plans, NEST is designed to keep management rates low and spread investment risks among a large membership. The fund is expected to have more than 8 million members.

Canadian defined contribution pension members could benefit significantly from aspects of the Australian and British approach. Automatic enrolment could turn millions of under-savers into pension members. More importantly, they could expect to accumulate bigger savings through lower management fees. Canadians who invest their defined contribution savings in mutual funds are paying significantly more in fees than their counterparts in Australia, the United Kingdom, and the United States. According to a recent study, Canadian investors pay average annual management and trailer fees equal to

3.43 per cent of invested assets. The fee is as much as 40 per cent higher than similar rates in the other countries and several times the typical defined benefit pension fund management expense ratio of 0.4 per cent.[9]

At a time when real investment returns are projected to remain in the low single digits, lower management fees could significantly increase pension savings. A recent British study estimated that the country's pension members were losing nearly 40 per cent of their savings over the lifetime of their pensions by paying a standard annual fee of 1.5 per cent.[10] Under the current Canadian rate structure, the damage is even greater. It is hard to think of a more compelling motivation for reform.

There are aspects of two other Canadian reform proposals that we believe could improve the pension coverage of existing or new defined contribution plans. Toronto pension consultant and adviser Keith Ambachtsheer advocates a nationwide pension that could strengthen the retirement savings of those with inadequate pensions or savings. He proposes a new pension model, called the Canada supplementary pension plan (CSPP). Like British and Australian reforms, he proposes that employees be automatically enrolled but allowed to opt out.

What is unique about the CSPP proposal is that it addresses longevity risks through the use of an insurance product known as a deferred annuity. From the age of forty-five, for example, employees would automatically invest a small portion of their pension savings each year for the next two decades. The end result would be an annuity that would guarantee a fixed monthly payment for life after retirement, eliminating much of the investment and longevity risks associated with standard defined contribution plans.

This plan is similar to the U.S.–based Teachers Insurance and Annuity Association—College Retirement Equities Fund (TIAA-CREF), which was founded in the early 1900s to provide retirement security for university professors. Although the current Canadian annuity market is small, we believe providers will emerge to meet market demand. Another option is for pension funds to follow the TIAA-CREF model and supply annuities internally.

Quebec recently proposed a new pension concept that could be applied to defined contribution plans to extend retirement benefits for longer-living retirees. An expert Quebec committee proposed in the spring of 2013 a "longevity pension" that could bridge retirement income gaps.[11] The committee concluded that half the province's middle-income households are not saving enough to replace 60 per cent of their incomes after retirement. To shield the province from the consequences of widespread income declines, the committee proposed a compulsory pension that would operate alongside the Quebec Pension Plan and whose assets would be managed by the Caisse de dépôt et placement du Québec. The committee suggested employees and employers split the cost of a 3.3 per cent contribution rate to fund the longevity pension. Unlike the QPP and CPP, which start paying full benefits at age sixty-five, the longevity pension does not kick in until seventy-five. The later benefit date and mandatory pension savings is an inducement for workers to accumulate more savings and extend their work years beyond sixty-five.

There is an abundance of innovative ideas to improve defined contribution plans. They will not be effective pension savings plans unless membership is mandatory and they have sufficient scale to engage professional investment managers and reduce risks and costs. Also essential are new financial products to insulate at least a portion of retirement savings from market volatility.

Touching the Third Rail

Public policy issues posed by pension reforms aren't complicated. Our governments must decide whether the costs of implementing new pension tiers and plan enhancements outweigh the economic damage inflicted when millions of Canadian households experience severe income declines after retirement. It is inescapable that Canadian taxpayers and younger workers will be left with the pension bill if we don't repair threatened or inadequate pension plans. While we bury our heads in the sand, visionary political and, in some cases, labour and business leaders in the United Kingdom, Australia, the Netherlands, Rhode Island, and even one of our frailest provinces, New Brunswick, have summoned the political courage to redesign wounded pension systems. They have taken these steps before waves of baby boom retirees place unsustainable burdens on pension plans and government budgets. Rhode Island has taught us the devastating perils of waiting too long to repair crumbling pension schemes.

Most of the proposals we have highlighted do not involve significant changes to Canada's existing pension regimes. They are additions or enhancements to government and workplace systems that are mostly already in place. New federal and provincial legislation would be needed to change the structure and governance of existing plans. New laws would encourage greater workplace participation in pensions, higher savings rates, and a more effective fund management system.

Canada must also address its weak system of pension regulation. Federally registered pension plans are overseen by the Superintendent of Financial Institutions, which has its hands full regulating the country's banks, insurers, and other financial players. The majority of our pension plans are regulated by the provinces, which pay limited attention to how private and public sector plans are governed. There are so many gaps in this system that pension plans continue to overstate the funding health of their funds by applying outdated assumptions about mortality rates and unrealistic investment projections. As pension costs rise, these lax practices weaken the health of funds when they are most needed to finance rising pensions costs.

Adding another layer of unnecessary regulatory confusion is our federal tax code. Existing tax laws are interfering with public policy aspirations for fairer and more effective retirement savings systems. For example, due to a Canada Revenue Agency (CRA) rule quirk, members of defined benefit plans currently have more room to invest in RRSPs than employees belonging to weaker defined contribution plans. Some tax rules are so inflexible that they stand in the way of pension innovation. In recent years some corporate pension sponsors have abandoned efforts to create new and innovative hybrid pension plans because of resistance from the CRA. For years, federal tax rules effectively prevented pension funds from building large surpluses to fortify pension plans. Although these rules were recently relaxed, our pension plans are still living with the legacy of funding damage.

We can borrow another lesson from the Dutch: pension reform today must be a continuous exercise. The tradition of large reforms every few decades no longer makes sense in an era of so much market and economic volatility. Modern pension plans need to be given more legal and structural flexibility to innovate in the face of constant changes. We also believe that our federal and provincial governments have to devote more resources to monitoring the health of this essential industry.

There is one final and essential reform. We as a society need to adjust our attitudes to pensions. We have little to gain by acting like the vengeful Russian farmer who wants neighbours to be punished for his own misfortunes. Pension envy and pension bashing is counterproductive. Pensions can work. It is true that Canada's large public and private sector pension funds are confronting funding challenges. Our pension plans were not built to accommodate so many greying and long-living boomers. And unsteady markets can no longer make up for these structural failures. But none of these weaknesses have to be fatal if we repair them now. We have highlighted many affordable solutions for reviving our ailing pension system: enhancing the CPP to address middle-income earners, arresting the decline of defined benefit plans, and building more effective defined contribution plans. If we ignore these reforms, we will bequeath future taxpayers and workers with a pension bill that inevitably no one can afford. The solution to our crisis is smarter pension coverage, not less.

ACKNOWLEDGEMENTS

Canada's growing pension debate has attracted many diligent rescue workers. Some have tirelessly mined demographic, economic, and corporate statistics for years to warn us about the consequences of an inadequate and unsustainable pension system. Others are devoted to building new models. All have persevered in the face of political paralysis toward one of the leading socio-economic problems of our time.

Many of these pension experts generously shared their time, research, and ideas with the authors, and we are deeply indebted to them. At the top of the list is a core group of past and present senior executives at Ontario Teachers' Pension Plan. During his tenure as Teachers' inaugural chief executive officer (1990–2007), Claude Lamoureux fostered a culture of innovation that saw Teachers' trail-blaze investment innovations, member services, benefit reforms, and shareholder rights. Furthermore, chair Eileen Mercier recognized years ago the crucial role the plan should play in the public pension debate. It takes progressive thinking to make the changes needed to ensure pension plan sustainability. Teachers' sponsors have led the field with tough decisions for the long-term benefit of its 300,000 members. This was possible because of the leadership of Ontario Teachers' Federation (particularly Maureen Davis, Ken Coran, and Rhonda Kimberley-Young) and the Ontario government, represented by Ross Peebles.

We are also grateful for the support of three senior Teachers' executives: Barbara Zvan, Melissa Kennedy and Ken Harrison. They challenged the authors' ideas and spied untold errors and omissions in early drafts. Equally important was Deborah Allan, Teachers' director of communications, who pushed for this book and was an indispensable midwife during its gestation and birth. The views and opinions expressed in this book are the personal views and opinions of the authors and do not necessarily reflect those of OTPP.

A core fraternity of pension experts and consultants patiently shared their time and knowledge to assist us with this book. We would like to thank Keith Ambactsheer, Bob Baldwin, and Hugh Mackenzie. Bill Walker and Dean Cooke helped navigate a unique and seamless collaboration between a pension plan chief executive and business journalist. Many others shared their time, research, and a steady stream of pension research updates: Janet McFarland, Bill Cole, Nelson Joannette, Allan Shapira, Jason Malone, Ian McSweeney, Malcolm Hamilton, Harry Arthurs, Bruce Kennedy, and the thorough staff in Teachers' Knowledge Centre.

In our travels to different regimes, many local pension guides went out of their way to escort us through a jungle of local laws, politics, and stories. The bulk of information in our chapters on New Brunswick, Rhode Island, and the Netherlands was drawn from lengthy interviews with government, labour, and pension advisers. In New Brunswick, we would like to thank Premier David Alward, Paul McCrossan, Sue Rowland, Pierre-Marcel Desjardins, Marilyn Quinn, Susie Proulx-Daigle, and John Ferguson. In Rhode Island, we were greatly assisted by Gina Raimondo, Joy Fox, Gayle Corrigan, Robert Flanders, Michael Downey, Bruce Ogni, and John Hill. In the Netherlands, Theo Kocken, Dirk Broeders, Eduard Ponds, Chris Driessen, and Niels Kortleve proved enormous help. A big assist came from Teachers' Linda Webster, who helped co-ordinate much of the travel logistics.

We would like to thank McClelland & Stewart editor Doug Pepper for his patience as we tested the very tight deadline for this book. Thank you also to Heather Sangster and Bhavna Chauhan for their nimble edits of the book.

It is impossible to write a book without the enormous understanding, patience, and support of family. The unsung heroes in this book were the authors' spouses. Jim Leech would like to thank Deborah Barrett for keeping him grounded and on track. Jacquie McNish is thankful to Stephen Cole, who shouldered extra parental duties with grace and thoughtfully edited the first draft of the book.

Jim Leech
Jacquie McNish
July 2013

ENDNOTES

CHAPTER 1

1. Nelson Joannette, *Worn Out: The Origins and Early Development of Pensions in Canada* (Waterloo, ON: University of Waterloo, 1993), 179.
2. Roger Lowenstein, *While America Aged*, (New York: Penguin Books, 2008), 25.
3. Peter Drucker, *The Unseen Revolution; How Pension Fund Socialism Came to America* (New York: Harper & Row, 1976), 132.
4. Elizabeth Shilton, "*Gifts or Rights? A Legal History of Employment Pension Plans in Canada,*" (Toronto: University of Toronto, 2011) 93.
5. Larry French, "Born in Tumult: Now a Pension Giant," *Education Forum* 37, no. 3 (Fall 2011): 17.
6. Jim Oeppen and James Vaupel, "Broken Limits to Life Expectancy," *Science Magazine* Vol. 296 no. 5570 (May 10, 2002): 1029-1031.
7. Statistics Canada, "Centenarians in Canada," *2011 Census in Brief*, catalogue no. 98-311-X2011003, 2012. 1.

8. Certified General Accountants Association of Canada, *Gauging the Path of Private Canadian Pensions*, 2010, 11.
9. Hugh Mackenzie, *Canada's Broken Retirement Income System: What's Next?* Centre for Labour Management Relations, Ryerson University, November 26, 2012, 4.
10. Keith Horner, Research Working Group on Income Adequacy, Department of Finance Canada, December 1, 2009.
11. Boston Consulting Group, *Measuring the Impact of Canadian Pension Funds*, February 11, 2013.
12. Boston Consulting Group, *Defined Benefit Impact Assessment*, June 6, 2013.

CHAPTER 2

1. Esther Clark Wright, *Loyalists of New Brunswick* (Moncton: Moncton Publishing Co. Ltd., 1955), 77.
2. Lori McLeod, "Pension Shortfall Leaves a Town Divided," *National Post*, October 4, 2006., 6.
3. One of the hardship cases Bernard Richard cited in his report concerned a husband and wife who had worked a combined forty-eight years at the mill and accrued more than $200,000 in future pension benefits. Younger than the cut-off age of fifty-five for pension protection, the husband and wife were only

eligible to each claim $10,000 before the provincial laws was changed. "They are mad, disillusioned and very fearful of their economic future and a rough road ahead." Bernard Richard, "Complaints from Former Employees and Retirees of the Nackawic Mill," November 14, 2005. 4.

4. Justice William Grant, Case 2011 NBQB 182, *Quinn et al v. Province of New Brunswick*, July 8, 2011, 9.
5. M. David Brown, "Public Role of Actuaries in Private Pensions in Canada," *North American Actuarial Journal* 3, no. 4 (October 1999).
6. Mr. Justice H. H. McLellan, Ruling, *Board of Trustee of the City of Saint John et al. v. Ferguson*, May 17, 2007.
7. The libel case cost an estimated $5 million in legal fees for the city and Ferguson. Most of the costs were covered by Saint John's insurance policy.

CHAPTER 3

1. Robert Grieve, *An Illustrated History of Pawtucket and Central Falls and Vicinity* (Providence: Henry R. Caufield, 1897), 165.
2. Rhode Island Public Expenditure Council, *Fiscal Stress and Municipal Bankruptcy: History and Implications for Rhode Island*, April, 2012, 3.
3. Paul Solman, Public Pension Problems: a Tale of Two Cities in Rhode Island," PBS, March 4, 2011.

4. Ibid.
5. Gina Raimondo, *Truth in Numbers: The Security and Sustainability of Rhode Island's Retirement System*, Office of the Treasurer of Rhode Island, May 2011, 3.
6. Mary Williams Walsh, "The Little State With a Big Mess," *The New York Times*, Oct. 22, 2011.
7. Michael McDonald, "Gina Raimondo Math Convinces Rhode Island of America's Prospects," *Bloomberg*, Jan. 10, 2012.
8. U.S. Government Accountability Office, *State and Local Government Pension Plans*, March 2012, 13.
9. Paul Burton, "Central Falls Fiscal Woes Resonate," *The Bond Buyer*, August 8, 2011, 3.
10. John Hill, "Central Falls: For City, Decades of Missed Chances," *Providence Journal*, September 11, 2011.
11. After serving as Central Falls' mayor for nine years, Charles Moreau was sentenced to two years in prison in February 2013 after he pled guilty to a federal corruption charge related to a local home foreclosure contract granted to a political supporter.

CHAPTER 4

1. David Wilsford, *Political Leaders of Contemporary Western Europe: A Biographical Dictionary* (Westport, CT: Greenwood Press, 1995, p. 111.

2. Federation of Dutch Pension Funds, *Collectivity/ Solidarity: The Evolution and Position of Collective Pensions in the Netherlands*, 2011, 20.
3. Organisation for Economic Co-operation and Development, *OECD Economic Surveys: Netherlands*, June 2012, 16.
4. Federation of Dutch Pension Funds, 48.
5. Wendel Broere, "Dutch Pension Agency Unveils Tighter Rules," Reuters, September 30, 2002.
6. International Monetary Fund, *Kingdom of the Netherlands-Netherlands: Publication of Financial Sector Assessment Program Documentation—Technical Note on Pensions Sector Issues*, July 2011, 21.
7. Dirk Broeders, Sylvester Eijffinger and Aerdt Houben, "*Frontiers in Pension Finance*," Edward Elgar Publishing, 2008, 308.
8. Federation of Dutch Pension Funds, p. 56A.

CHAPTER 5

1. Hugh Mackenzie, *Canada's Broken Retirement Income System: What's Next?* Centre for Labour Management Relations, Ryerson University, November 26, 2012, 6.
2. David Dodge, Alexandre Laurin, and Colin Busby, *The Piggy Bank Index: Matching Canadians' Saving*

Rates to Their Retirement Dreams, C.D. Howe Institute, March 18, 2010, 4.

3. Bob Baldwin, "Pension Reform in Canada; A Guide to Fixing Our Futures Again," *IRPP*, no. 13 (December 2010): 16.
4. Organisation for Economic Co-operation and Development, *Pension Markets in Focus*, no. 8 (July 2011): 10.
5. The data on Canada's defined benefit retirees were supplied by Boston Consulting Group in a June 2013 study *Defined Benefit Impact Assessment*. The study was commissioned by seven public sector pension plans.
6. Alicia Munnell, Jean-Pierre Aubry, Josh Hurwitz, and Laura Quinby, "A Role for Defined Contribution Plans in the Public Sector," Center for Retirement Research at Boston College Brief No. 16, April 2011: 2. Using 2008 data, the authors found expenses as a percent of assets in defined benefit plans were 0.43 per cent, compared with 0.95 per cent in defined contribution plans.
7. Michael Wong, commentary, *Telegraph Journal* (Saint John), April 2013.
8. William Morneau, *Facilitating Pooled Asset Management for Ontario's Public-Sector Institutions*, Report from the Pension Investment Advisor to the

Deputy Premier and Minister of Finance, October 2012, 14.

9. Keith Ambachtsheer, "Giving Mutual Fund Investors a Fair Shake: What It Will Take," Ambachtsheer letter, April 2013.
10. David Pitt-Watson, *Tomorrow's Investor: Building the Consensus for a People's Pension in Britain*, RSA Project, December 2010, 5.
11. Expert Committee on the Future of the Quebec Retirement System, *Innovating for a Sustainable Retirement System-Summary*, Second Quarter 2013, 30.